Policy Studies

One of the greatest achievements (add over 20 years to the average people. To survive into 'old age' is ne ...nority of people but an experience comm ... ..ajority. Retired people now constitute one-fifth of the population of the United Kingdom. *Policy Studies in Ageing* is a series of monographs which seeks to promote substantial contributions to public debate about policy issues which affect older members of society. These monographs are published by the Centre for Policy on Ageing, a registered charity established in 1947 to promote better policies for older people.

Policy Studies in Ageing is aimed at a wide readership amongst those in central and local government, the health authorities and voluntary bodies who are responsible for the formulation of policy or its implementation in practice. The series will also be of interest to those studying social policy or administration in universities and polytechnics and, it is hoped, to all who take an intelligent interest in the quality of their own later years.

Professor R.A.B. Leaper
Former Chairman, Advisory Council, Centre for Policy on Ageing

Other titles in the series
Alison Norman, *Mental illness in old age: meeting the challenge.* Policy Studies in Ageing no 1, 1982

Eric Midwinter, *Age is opportunity: education and older people.* Policy Studies in Ageing no 2, 1982

Alison Norman, *Triple jeopardy: growing old in a second homeland.* Policy Studies in Ageing no 3, 1985

Eric Midwinter, *The wage of retirement: the case for a new pensions policy.* Policy Studies in Ageing no 4, 1985

Alan Norton, Bryan Stoten and Hedley Taylor, *Councils of care: planning a local government strategy for older people.* Policy Studies in Ageing no 5, 1986

Hedley Taylor, *Growing old together: elderly owner-occupiers and their housing.* Policy Studies in Ageing no 6, 1986

Alison Norman, *Severe dementia: the provision of longstay care.* Policy Studies in Ageing no 7, 1987

Susan Tester, *Caring by day: a study of day care services for older people.* Policy Studies in Ageing no 8, 1989

Policy Studies in Ageing
no 1

Mental illness in old age:
meeting the challenge

Alison Norman

Centre for Policy on Ageing

First published in 1982 by the
Centre for Policy on Ageing
25–31 Ironmonger Row
London EC1V 3QP

© 1982 Centre for Policy on Ageing
  Reprinted 1984, 1989
  Preface © 1989 Centre for Policy on Ageing

ISBN 0 904139 29 8

Printed in Great Britain by
Henry Ling Ltd, The Dorset Press, Dorchester, Dorset, England

Contents

Preface

Service provision in the field of psychogeriatrics has expanded greatly since this policy study was written in 1981. The number of consultant psychiatrists working five or more sessions in old age psychiatry has nearly doubled to 203 and 70% of the UK population now have access to some form of specialised service.[1] Specialist community psychiatric nurses are recognised as an essential and vital resource. Multi-disciplinary teams working in the field have become commonplace. Travelling day hospitals, weekend, evening and night-time care, and a variety of sitting-in services are beginning to make their value felt. Local specialist residential care provided by health, social services, and the private sector offers an alternative to the much more drastic segregation of long-stay psychiatric hospital wards.[2]

So why is a reprint of this policy study with its now rather faded examples of good practice needed? It is because the issues which it discusses are just as valid as they were when it was first published. Certainly service provision has expanded, but a third of the health districts still have no specialist consultants and most are still grossly under-resourced. Many specialist consultant posts remain unfilled because there are no candidates who have received the necessary training. The psychiatry of old age is still not recognised as a specialty within psychiatry so that money, personnel and training places which should be used in this field cannot be properly identified and defended. There is no effective mechanism to ensure that the resources released by the closure of the Victorian psychiatric hospitals are channelled towards intensive community support and community-level facilities. The 'challenge' therefore is still a long way from being met.

Nowhere is this more obvious than in the 'awful separation' which still exists almost everywhere between health and social services provision. At field level there is sometimes excellent mutual support and some joint activity but this is because of the initiative of concerned and charismatic individuals. When it comes to sharing resources in any genuinely joint service, however, virtually no progress has been made. Indeed, straitened revenue funding is guarded even more jealously than it has been in the past. Also, within both health and social services, chasms still yawn between provision for elderly people and provision for people with mental illness, and minimal allowance is made for the needs of the vast majority of mentally-disabled elderly people who need special and skilled support and care but who can still share in many of the 'ordinary' activities of their age group and who benefit greatly by doing so.

Finally, something needs to be said about the private sector which was in its infancy when this study was first published. The sharp rise in the numbers of the very old has provided the clientele for a massive increase in DSS-funded private residential and nursing home care. Many of these residents are admitted with dementia or chronic functional illness. Many more develop dementia and depression while in care. Proprietors and staff are often not trained to cope except by using heavy sedation, and the restrictions on DSS income support make it impossible to staff homes to the level required by heavily dependent people. Both health and social services are usually reluctant to take over residents who are rejected by private homes and relatives are often desperate in their hunt for alternative placements or in their struggle to meet the demand for increased fees. During the 1980s the private sector has bailed out both health and social services. There will be disastrous results for this very vulnerable client group if they are expected to continue to do so without fees which properly reflect levels of dependency, without management and staff training which reflects this highly skilled task, and without a genuine cooperative partnership with health and social services professionals. Already people who are suitable for residential care but who cannot find affordable places are again 'silting up' the long-term hospital beds. Fears of inadequate funding of highly intensive 'community care' under the Griffiths proposals make the future seem even more bleak.

And yet, as this report says, 'the cause is not hopeless nor the pit bottomless. This is a field in which a reasonable injection of skill, optimism, determination and funding can provide a reasonable and viable service'. The immense expansion of interest in old age psychiatry in all the relevant professions during the 1980s is an immensely hopeful sign. High quality writing and research is being carried out. The Royal Colleges of Physicians and Psychiatrists have united to press that the psychiatry of old age should become a specialty[3]; the King's Fund Centre has put its immense prestige behind a report which maintains the rights and the value of dementia sufferers[4]; and it is now recognised that 'specialist' long-term care can be a synonym for 'the best possible care' rather than a euphemism for 'a sin-bin of social rejects'.[5] The Alzheimer's Disease Society is gaining strength, recognition and influence.[6] The Open University is running a training course for professionals who want to improve their knowledge of this field.[7] Changes in the law have marginally improved elderly people's rights and it is now possible to sign an 'enduring power of attorney' which is valid 'when the donor ceases to be mentally competent'.[8]

We still have an immense way to go but we have gone a long way since this report was written. It is to be hoped that by the time this edition is sold out it will be too outdated to be worth reprinting.

REFERENCES
1. J P Wattis, Geographical variations in the provision of psychiatric services for old people, *Age and Ageing*, 1988, 17, 3, 171–80.
2. A Norman, *Severe dementia: the provision of longstay care*, Centre for Policy on Ageing, London, 1987.
3. *Care of elderly people with mental illness: specialist services and medical training*, Joint Report of the Royal College of Physicians and the Royal College of Psychiatrists, London, 1989.
4. *Living well into old age: applying principles of good practice to services for people with dementia*, King's Fund Centre, London, 1986.
5. See ref. 2.
6. Alzheimer's Disease Society, 158/160 Balham High Road, London SW12 9BN.
7. The Open University course *Mental Health Problems in Old Age* is the third of three short courses developed as part of the *Education for Health* project by the Department of Health and Social Welfare. Intending students can obtain further particulars from the Department of Health and Social Welfare, The Open University, Walton Hall, Milton Keynes MK7 6AA.
8. These legal changes are summarised in the foreword to the 1987 edition of *Rights and risk: a discussion document on civil liberty in old age*, Alison Norman, Centre for Policy on Ageing, 1980.

Foreword

CPA has chosen mental illness in old age as the subject of the first in the *Policy Studies in Ageing* series because it is an issue which is basic to all other aspects of successful ageing and good service provision. Good mental health is essential for good self care, and good services are essential to provide the early and efficient diagnosis, treatment and support which are needed to maintain such health at the maximum possible level. Yet, in both health and social services, provision is too often *ad hoc,* unplanned and piecemeal, and elderly people with mental disability are shunted around like a game of 'pass the parcel'—ignored, unwanted and often totally neglected. It would have been easy to write a review drawing attention to the worst aspects of neglect, but it would not have been very helpful. Instead, this study seeks to illustrate what can be done and is being done to provide imaginative caring and cost effective services in this field, and then to discuss the policy issues underlying such service provision. The examples are based principally on journal articles and on visits to a varied but inevitably limited number of service providers who are doing innovative or unusual work in this field.

Readers may wonder why 'mental illness' rather than 'confusion' or 'mental infirmity' figures in the title and throughout the report, when the stigma attached to mental illness is still so strong. It is because I believe that the very strength of that stigma has engendered the proliferation of kindly-meant but unhelpful euphemisms which encourage failure to investigate, diagnose, treat, or plan for care. 'To confuse' according to the *Concise Oxford Dictionary,* is to 'throw into disorder; to mix up in the mind; to abash; or to perplex'. To say that someone is confused gives no indication about the cause of his or her condition. I may be confused because I have woken in an unfamiliar room on a dark night and cannot find the light-switch, or because I am trying to study mathematics and cannot grasp the principles of calculus. Similarly, to say that someone is 'mentally infirm' says as little about the nature of the disability or the severity of the symptoms as describing someone as 'physically infirm' would do. I am very far from claiming that because mental disability is an illness it is the sole province of the medical profession, but I do claim that we will make very little progress in providing treatment or care until we face facts. If there is no illness, there is no cause of malfunctioning and therefore no cause for concern. If there is illness, then we need to know what is causing it and what can be done about it.

Problems of terminology occur again in referring to the specialist study and practice of old age psychiatry. The words 'psychogeriatric' and 'psychogeriatrician' have become unpopular because they are too often taken to refer only to specialists in dementia. However, it seems defeatist to allow perfectly good and convenient words to go out of use because they are subject to misuse by the ignorant. The World Health Organization in 1972 stated that 'psychogeriatrics is a branch of psychiatry concerned with all the mental disorders of old age, but particularly with those that first emerge as significant at the age of 65 years. Psychogeriatrics is concerned with the various forms of mental disorder in old age, their epidemiology, origin, prevention, development and treatment'. It is in this broad sense that these words are used in this report.

Finally, the limitations of the English language make it necessary to say a word about the use of pronouns. The lack of a neutral pronoun in the third person singular forces any writer either to use one gender throughout or to resort to the clumsy 'he or she' or to make an arbitrary choice. Reluctantly, I have settled for the third option, as being the least obtrusive. Thus, doctors are 'he' and patients, social workers, nurses and care staff are 'she' except where the context demands otherwise. Inevitably this usage reinforces stereotypes and readers are asked to keep in mind the many female psychiatrists and male nurses and social workers who are contributing in this field and the many elderly men who suffer from mental illness.

Acknowledgements

In the course of compiling this report, visits were made to over 60 institutions and interviews held with at least twice that number of individuals. For that reason, it is not possible to name all the people who showed me what they were doing and who talked about their work, but I wish to record my thanks to them all for their willing co-operation. Some are named individually where it seemed appropriate to do so in the text, but no slight is intended to those whose work and views are cited anonymously in the report. I have tried to represent their work and their opinions accurately, but over-simplification is inevitably in danger of creeping in when discussing such a complex subject, and I apologise if this has occurred.

Grateful thanks are also due to the Department of Health and Social Security which awarded a grant towards the cost of the study.

Alison Norman, July 1982

1 Mental illness in old age

Forty years ago, physically-ill elderly people were assumed to be suffering from the irreversible effects of old age. They were tucked up in bed and looked after until the original cause of their illness, or pneumonia, or mental and physical atrophy produced the expected death usually after a long period of increasing disability and misery. Thanks to the pioneers of geriatric medicine and their successors, as well as to major advances in medical knowledge and surgical techniques, this is, in theory at least, no longer true. Physically-ill elderly people are treated or operated on at any age. Their fractured femurs are expertly pinned, their muscles retrained and their capacity for self-care restored whenever possible. If it were not so, the health and social services would be totally unable to cope with the strain put upon them. With regard to mental illness in old age, however, we are still emerging from the dark ages. Symptoms are described as if the description was a diagnosis. Old people are called 'senile', 'confused', 'mentally infirm', or 'geriatric' and the label is then used to condemn them to a limbo existence in which recognition of identity, personality, civic rights and human needs disappears in a miasma of professional hopelessness.

These attitudes are beginning—just beginning—to change. We now recognise that old age is a time of mental as well as physical vulnerability. It is often a time of bereavement, financial anxiety and loss of role which can, in turn, generate disorientation, social isolation and malnutrition. Complex combinations of physical and environmental factors can induce deep depression which is often manifested in anxiety, apathy, agitation and self-neglect. Physical illness or inappropriate medication easily produces a confusional state. And any of these conditions may be exacerbated by the assumption that 'it's old age', that 'nothing can be done', that 'she is not fit to look after herself' so that the original illness is complicated by loss of independence, loss of a familiar and loved home and loss of daily routine. Thus, as with a physically-ill old person who is allowed to become bedfast, social expectation often becomes a self-fulfilling prophecy.

Very old age is also a time of special vulnerability to illnesses which cause organic brain damage with consequent increasingly severe loss of short-term memory, loss of capacity for self-care and, in some cases, changes of personality and inappropriate social behaviour. It has only very recently been fully accepted that these dementias are not part of the ordinary processes of ageing and that they are caused by a complex syndrome of disease processes relating to the chemistry of the brain or the blood supply to brain cells. The scientific research which is beginning to give hope of eventually preventing or treating these conditions has coincided with the realisation that social and medical disinterest has generated such profound neglect of dementia-sufferers and their carers that symptoms have often been allowed to become more severe and more socially disabling than is necessary. Early intervention, proper diagnosis and a clear plan for care can, we now realise, be of very positive benefit.

It is against this background that we are beginning to see a strong and growing interest in the psychogeriatric field. During the last two years, for example, MIND has produced a number of publications in this field.[1] The Office of Health Economics has published a succinct and informative booklet summarising the available statistical and research information on dementia.[2] The Royal College of Physicians has produced a formal report on the implications of organic mental impairment in old people for research, education and the provision of services.[3] A number of books have been published which are addressed to general readership and encourage proper understanding, assessment and treatment of elderly people with mental disability.[4] Also, organisations such as the Equal Opportunities Commission have called attention to the severe physical, social and financial cost borne by families who care for a heavily dependent relative and the likelihood, for complex social and demographic reasons, that the number of people who are able and willing to take on this burden full-time will rapidly decrease.[5]

One primary reason for this sudden spurt of interest must be that the weight of the need is finally getting through to the service providers. Prophecy, based on epidemiological studies and demographic evidence of the rapidly growing 75 + age group, is one thing. Battling with desperate relatives, overcrowded and understaffed wards and unsuitable residential care facilities is quite another. In sheer self-defence, the service providers are having to give more than token acknowledgement to the 'problem'. Another and more positive aspect is the development of serious and informed professional interest by psychiatrists in the psychiatry of old age. Psychogeriatric 'centres of excellence' are still too rare, but as this report makes clear, they do exist and are staffed by people who have not only commitment and concern, but a high level of knowledge and ability. Another new development is the interest which professional social workers and social work teachers are beginning to take in this field, following the rebirth of specialisation in social work departments. Also, relevant voluntary organisations are beginning to realise they have a valuable contribution to offer. There is a long way to go, but the atmosphere is certainly very different to that of the beginning of the seventies.

Over against this stirring of interest and optimism must be set the very powerful deadweight of resentment, hopelessness and sheer inertia which still bedevils the professional, administrative and political response to the health needs of the elderly. In physical medicine, we are accustomed, unfortunately, to the misuse of 'geriatric' as an abusive term to describe someone who is not worth the trouble of treating; to the paucity of research on the common crippling disorders of old age; to the neglect and resentment of elderly people considered to be 'blocking beds' in acute wards; and to the edge which the acute medical specialisms maintain over chronic illness in the fight for resources. If all this is true in the geriatric field, it is trebly so in psychogeriatrics. The elderly mentally-ill and especially those who, rightly or wrongly, have been labelled as suffering from dementia, are commonly seen as a bottomless pit, swallowing up resources which would be far better spent on prevention and treatment in younger age groups. It is a prime objective of this report to show that the cause is *not* hopeless nor the pit bottomless, although the size of the challenge in sheer weight of numbers cannot be denied. During the last quarter of the century, the number of people aged over 74 is expected to increase by three-quarters of a million, most of this growth occurring in the next fifteen years. The steepest increase, however, will be in the very old. Between 1976 and 2001, the number of people in England and Wales aged over 85 is projected to increase by nearly a third of a million to 775 000.[6] Areas which already have a high concentration of elderly people will carry a still heavier responsibility. For example, East Sussex already has over 24% of its population aged over 65 (compared with a national average of 15·1%) and 10% of its population is over 75. The Isle of Wight, West Sussex and Devon all have more than 19% over 65 and more than 7% over 75.

These are frightening figures, in view of the mental vulnerability of the very old, but there is ample evidence that if a reasonable basic level of resources is provided, if adequate training and support is given, and if all the relevant bodies and professions are prepared to pull their weight, instead of doing their utmost to disclaim responsibility, the challenge *can* be met. It is the failure to provide basic resources and to accept responsibility which creates an intolerable burden by generating chronic dependency and the collapse of overburdened support systems. Every failure to recover normally from a bereavement—every unrecognised depression which generates apathy, self-neglect and despair—every acute confusional state which is mis-diagnosed as dementia—every family which is swamped by the strain of caring for an elderly relative—is a seedbed for acute social problems and social breakdown which may lead to long-term care becoming inescapable. Early and effective intervention is vital if our services are to cope.

Such intervention cannot be regarded as the responsibility of any one service or profession. It demands, as this report seeks to illustrate, an informed, enthusiastic and co-operative effort from everyone who comes into contact with mental suffering in old age. The report is, therefore, addressed not only to a handful of informed specialists, but to GPs, social workers, community nurses, volunteers, home helps, residential care staff, planners, administrators, hospital staff (from consultants to porters), and of course to the friends and relatives without whose sacrificial support the professionals are helpless. It is a basic theme of the argument that we are under-using and mis-using the resources which we have, and that carers of every kind have far more skill and understanding to offer than the present system allows them to give. But to release this reservoir of help, pump-priming in terms of staffing, training and accommodation is also essential. It is simply not sensible to go on trying to meet the exploding need by spreading the present provision more and more thinly. Inevitably there comes a point when no-one, whether struggling relative, exhausted care staff, sleepless sheltered-housing warden, disillusioned nurse or despairing doctor, can go on coping. The battle against mental illness in old age cannot be won without basic equipment. This report attempts to indicate where the injection of extra resources is most needed and will be most cost effective.

Finally, the point needs to be made that obtaining help is a two-way process. It has to be asked for as well as given, and the glib labels which we attach to mental disorder in old age may make asking for help at the right time extremely difficult. Old people who are aware that their brains are not functioning properly may go to great lengths to disguise this fact with all its attendant fears. Depression may be disguised by preoccupation with physical symptoms or be accepted as a natural response to bereavement and physical disability. Relatives may fear that if they ask for medical help, matters will be taken out of their hands entirely or just assume that 'it's old age' and that nothing can be done. The guilt and shame which has now, to some extent, lost its association with mental illness in younger age groups still clings to the old. And if the illness in question is a true dementia, lack of understanding about the effects of memory loss and resulting hurt and bewilderment may compound this shame and increase the desire for concealment. We need to strengthen the community's response to requests for help, but we also need to improve public education in recognising when help is needed and should be asked for.

REFERENCES
1. *Mental health of elderly people – MIND's response to the DHSS discussion paper 'A happier old age'.* MIND, London, 1979.
Positive approaches to mental infirmity in elderly people: MIND's annual conference report, October 1978. MIND, London, 1979.
Tony Whitehead, *A ripe old age.* MIND, London, 1979.
David Plank and Sheila Peace, *What next for elderly people? An overview of service provision and research concerning elderly mentally infirm people.* MIND, London, 1979.
2. *Dementia in old age.* Office of Health Economics, London, 1979.
3. Organic mental impairment in the elderly: implications for research, education and the provision of services; a report of the Royal College of Physicians by the College Committee on Geriatrics. *Journal of the Royal College of Physicians of London,* 15, 3, 1981, 141–167.
4. J A Muir Gray and Heather McKenzie, *Take care of your elderly relative,* George Allen and Unwin and Beaconsfield Publishers, London, 1980.
Barbara Gray and Bernard Isaacs, *Care of the elderly mentally infirm.* Tavistock Publications, London, 1980.
Tim Dartington, *Family care of old people.* Souvenir Press, London, 1980.
5. Equal Opportunities Commission, *The experience of caring for elderly and handicapped dependants: survey report.* EOC, Manchester, 1980.
6. *Population projections 1979–2019.* Office of Population Censuses and Surveys. HMSO, London, 1981.

2 The 'need'

Inevitably, this report focuses on the mental vulnerability of elderly people and the services and treatment which are needed to safeguard their mental health. However, it is necessary to emphasise at the outset that the vast majority of elderly people remain mentally well and with vigorously functioning minds until their death. Pensioners form a large proportion of students catered for in adult education classes, for example; 2700 students over 60 are on the books of the Open University; the concept of the University of the Third Age is arousing widespread interest; members of professions which do not have a fixed retirement age often continue to practice with undiminished vigour into their seventies and eighties; and an enormous range of voluntary work is organised and carried out by older people. When we are told that 22% of people over eighty are likely to suffer from some degree of dementia, it is as well to remember that in that case 78% of people in their eighties will have no organic brain disorder. As Longfellow reminds us in *Morituri Salutamus*

> Ah, nothing is too late
> Till the tired heart shall cease to palpitate.
> Cato learned Greek at eighty; Sophocles
> Wrote his grand Oedipus, and Simonides
> Bore off the prize of verse from his compeers,
> When each had numbered more than fourscore years.

All too often accidents or forgetfulness are attributed to old age when in a younger person they would be regarded as amusing or tiresome mishaps. There can be few people who have not burned out a kettle or forgotten to turn off a tap at some time in their lives. We all experience mental blanks when a well-known name or telephone number suddenly eludes us. Some of us have been hopeless all our lives at remembering faces or doing mental arithmetic. Yet when an elderly person floods the bathroom or muddles her change, or lets a saucepan burn dry, people start asking 'Is it safe for her to be alone?' and 'What if she should start a fire?' If there is serious evidence that something is amiss, then a proper assessment is necessary, but older people need the same latitude to make mistakes as members of any other age group. Similarly, they have the right to be sad, bad-tempered, unsociable or eccentric without being labelled as 'mentally infirm'. The enforced proximity engendered by physical dependence may make such characteristics in old people more obvious, and more tiresome or worrying, but they are not symptoms of illness and they merit a direct and honest response rather than a patronising assumption that 'She can't help it, poor old dear—it's her age'.

Having made that point, it must be admitted there is a 'grey' area where health and illness defy exact definition. This is true for physical health—most of us have experienced difficulty in deciding whether we really were ill enough to justify consulting a doctor or cancelling an engagement. It is doubly true for mental health in old age when the interaction of physical health, mental health, personality and environment makes precise definitions still more difficult. Indeed, the very complexity of mental malfunctioning in old age drives home the point, which is made again and again in this report, that thorough physical, psychiatric and social assessment is essential when someone is showing symptoms which give cause for concern. Assessment skills of this kind cannot be taught by the written word; they come from experience and from discussion with skilled practitioners. This chapter attempts only to outline the basic characteristics of the main psychiatric disorders of old age and to indicate the kind of treatment and support services which they demand in order to provide a foundation for the discussion in the rest of the report.

Acute confusional states
There are three groups of causes of acute confusional states. The first two are, respectively, physical illness and side effects from drugs and are more properly known as 'delirium'. The third is a sudden change in social situation or environment such as bereavement or change of dwelling or move to a hospital or residential home. These three causes can of course coincide and they may also be superimposed on a depression or dementia. It follows that when somebody seems confused in behaviour it is very important to make a thorough physical examination, and check for any unusual physical symptoms and also to look for any environmental reasons for stress.

Lodge lists the following as symptoms of an acute confusional state:[1]

A fluctuating alteration of mental activity. Mental activity becomes ill sustained: the person may for a short period talk appropriately, or maybe vaguely or inconsequentially. A few words only may be spoken. The talk may be of something quite irrelevant or out of context. Utterances may pursue a number of vaguely related or not obviously related topics very briefly one after another. The person may mutter to him or herself.

A fluctuating level of consciousness. The person is alert at times but this tends to alternate with periods of drowsiness. He or she goes in and out of sleep. The drowsiness and the altered mental activity are known collectively as a 'clouding of the consciousness'.

Poor concentration of thought. The patient is going in and out of a drowsy or sleepy state, so concentration is poor. Even when alert, concentration of ideas is difficult: the person's mind tends to wander.

Disorientation in time and space. The patient has difficulty in concentrating. At the same time, he or she is going in and out of a drowsy/sleepy state, and therefore loses track of what time it is, what day it is, where he or she is, and so on.

Muscular excitability. There tends to be great over-excitability of the body muscles. The patient in bed tends to pick at the bed clothes, folds them, wraps the bedding up into a ball. The hands tend to twitch. If the patient is touched, he or she may leap out of bed which makes nursing difficult. The person has to be approached slowly with explanations being given all the time, but may nevertheless cling onto the sheets or whatever is to hand. If the person is not in bed and the confusional state has come on more gradually, he or she may be described as restless. The person paces about; may be said to be wandering aimlessly; or may be actively engaged in some bizarre pursuit such as trying to open a drawer in the side of a desk where there are no drawers.

Misinterpretation of the environment and hallucinations. Shadows particularly may be misinterpreted; shapes may be misconstrued; noises may be thought to be other than they are. A small object on the floor—perhaps a bag—may be interpreted falsely as a black cat about to jump on the bed. Misinterpretations will be made during the day and night, although the night and darkness often exacerbate them. Sometimes however frank visual hallucinations may occur with no obvious stimulus. Such hallucinations and misinterpretations tend to evoke fear and even terror. The muscular irritability and these feelings of fear make nursing patients in an acute confusional state very difficult.

Depression
It is extremely difficult for the layman to grasp the concept of depression. One problem is that the word in common usage means 'sad', 'frustrated', 'fed up', 'bored', 'pessimistic'. These are normal

moods—often healthy reactions to life events. Clinical depression is another matter. The mood of someone with a depressive illness is much lower at his or her best moments than the mood of a normal person at his worst. As Lodge describes it:

'The mood of the *disease* depression is 'a terrible feeling'; life seems to have no purpose; everything takes on a gloomy, dark quality; there is an emptiness and a purposelessness; thoughts tend to be morbid and tinged with the stillness of death; time seems interminable, endless; there is no point to the future; there is a hopelessness in which everything seems stifled under a blanket of despair and gloom; there is an atmosphere of menacing lifelessness, an inert stillness everywhere. The person with the *disease* depression, however, rarely complains of the *symptom* depression.

In addition to the abnormal lowering of mood, there is a lowering of physical activity to a continuously abnormally low level. In some elderly people with depression agitation may be a prominent feature of the condition. The person then uses physical energy in such a manner that it is frittered away in useless or purposeless non-productive activity. Basically useful physical activity, however, is decreased. In the early stages of depression, the person may complain that everything is an effort, that it is impossible to get through work, and that he or she is just too tired to do things. The abnormal depth to which physical activity may be lowered can be such that the person just does not move; they remain slumped in a chair or in bed. The picture then looks like a picture of dementia and is, in fact, sometimes called a pseudo-dementia. The person does not move and finds the effort of going to the toilet too much, so is incontinent of urine (and possibly faeces). The person is sunk in thought with a deeply depressed mood as is described before, so that irrelevant questions like 'What day is it?', 'Who is the monarch?', 'Where are you?' seem so stupidly inane to the person that they are either ignored or answered incorrectly. The person is then erroneously believed to be definitely suffering from dementia.'

Other symptoms are feelings of guilt and unworthiness; acute irrational anxiety; concern about physical health; paranoid delusions and an altered sleep pattern. Depressed people often wake very early in the morning when their mood is also at its lowest ebb, and cannot get back to sleep again. This time is the highest suicidal risk point.

We do not know what causes depressive illness. It tends to run in families and is certainly related in some cases to childhood experience. It may be triggered by recent severe stress, but this is certainly not the sole factor or we would expect most old people to become depressed sooner or later. There may be a complex inter-relationship between stressful experiences and physical activity in the brain which gives rise to the symptoms and to which older people may be more susceptible than younger ones.[2] However that may be, it is certain that depressive illness is very common in old age and it is vital that it should be correctly diagnosed and treated. In less severe cases, anti-depressant medication from the GP will be effective while, for more severe illness which does not respond to drugs, or for patients who react with side-effects to drug therapy, electro-convulsive therapy (ECT) may be very effective. Some will recover without further relapses; some will have relapses, but be well in between them; some will continue to suffer from what Post calls 'depressed invalidism' as well as further acute attacks and some (about 10% of Post's in-patient sample) may remain in a state of chronic and unremitting depression. This is, however, a very small proportion of the population at risk and depression is an eminently treatable psychiatric condition.

Paraphrenia
This is a relatively uncommon illness which is thought to be a form of schizophrenia in the elderly, but which usually arises without any previous history of mental disorder. It is most common in single or widowed women, able to care for themselves, but socially isolated and with poor sight or hearing. The main symptom consists of one single fixed delusional idea which is not susceptible to any amount of argument and which relates to a conviction of being persecuted or sexually threatened. A sufferer may be convinced that her neigh-bours want to drive her out of her house or that they are sending X-rays at her from the flat upstairs or that the milkman is making sexual advances. Her response may be to attack back with a broom-handle on the ceiling or put grease on her neighbour's doorstep or complain to the police and the consequent furore then compounds the problem and probably reinforces her original conviction of per-secution with substantial evidence. People with this illness can often be persuaded to accept medication which they are told is to relieve their anxiety when they would certainly not accept any suggestion that they were ill, and suitable drugs can, in fact, damp down their symptoms. Measures to relieve isolation can also help, and the understanding of neighbours needs to be enlisted so that the delusions are not reinforced with actual retaliation. A combination

of medication and social support usually enables the situation to be contained even if it cannot be totally relieved.

Emotional disorders
The last third of life brings with it many stresses and changes which create emotional problems or exacerbate earlier tensions. Very old people have to come to terms with bereavement, with the fact of their nearing death, with the management of increasing physical dependency, perhaps with pain and disability, and with their changing role in their families and their wider society. Many will be lucky enough not to have to cope with these problems in an acute form and die after a short illness and a long life in which no real change has been forced upon them. Many others have the gift of coping without letting the difficulties change their personality or their relationships. But some do have difficulty in coming to terms with their experiences and this difficulty may be compounded by existing family relationships. Bergmann gives some examples.[3]

'A daughter having lived all her life with mother, adoring, dependent, seeking mother's advice on all issues and obeying all commands issued by mother, faces a change in this stable, benign tyranny due to illness, anxiety and depression coming on in the mother's old age. For the first time, mother is put into the dependent and subordinate position, but the daughter is not ready to assume command. Tensions arise as the daughter assumes more and more responsibility in the absence of real power and resentments on both sides may be acted out in very childlike ways.

Other patterns include that of the 'fallen dictator' and 'power reversal'. The fallen dictator may be a powerful domineering husband and father, good at his job, well thought of at work, but tyrannical, overbearing and oppressive at home, having always maintained his command by instilling fear. When ill health and loss of income and work status remove the actual basis of power and when increasing demands for help at home undermine his position, his tyrannical attempts to retain command in the face of a changing situation may well create crises and rejection by the rest of the family.

The opposite case is that of 'power reversal', where, so to speak, the worm turns. The man in this case may have been described as an 'ideal' husband, constantly helping in the household, handing over the wage packet unopened, not smoking, drinking or going out with his work mates, constantly working to improve the house, taking pleasure in carrying out the wishes of wife and children. He is usually viewed, when not being ignored, with amused contempt by his wife and family. In old age, this invaluable family member may develop a life-threatening illness, heart attack or a cancer, and for the first time his every move and symptom commands the attention of the whole family. If he survives his illness he may have learnt one lesson: that he has the power to frighten, stir up and to be the centre of attention. This lesson once learned, he may be loath to return to his previous humble status. From that moment war is on, and the old person, by every childish and regressive means, attempts to retain power. I have even seen one such man threaten to kick his wife's most precious china cabinet to bits if she did not obey his wishes!

Behind such scenes many forces must be at work. Struggles for power, emotional and physical dependencies, methods of rewarding behaviour and roles whose basis lies in childhood fantasies and struggles, rather than in current reality.'

Everyone working in this field needs to be aware of the possibility of tensions of this kind and their inter-relationship with past history and with current physical or mental illness. If the professional caregivers fail to recognise the dynamic issues behind a tense situation, they may try to treat the symptoms rather than the causes and offer solutions which only increase the anger, guilt and suffering endemic in the situation.

The dementias
The word 'dementia' is used to describe a syndrome in which 'there is a global impairment of memory and personality, but without impairment of consciousness'. It is entirely organic in origin, although it may be complicated by other forms of illness, and it is caused by malfunctioning which produces progressive, and in our present state of knowledge, unpreventable and irreversible, damage to the cerebral cortex. It is very important, as has been mentioned earlier, to be clear that this is an *illness* or group of illnesses which have nothing to do with the normal processes of ageing. It can attack people in middle-age, but becomes progressively more common as age increases, as is the case with many other diseases. The most quoted estimate of prevalence is based on surveys carried out in Newcastle in the 1960s which found that 6·2% of the population over 65 were suffering dementia of varying degrees of severity, the percentage rising from 2·8% in the 70–74 age group to 5·5% in the 75–79 age group and 22% in the over 80s. A number of other studies

have produced roughly similar percentages.[4] Given the nature of the illness and the very sharp rise in the number of the very old which was noted in the introduction these estimates are certainly a cause for very serious concern.

Among the elderly, the majority of people presenting with a dementing syndrome are suffering either from 'senile dementia of the Alzheimer type' (SDAT) or from multi-infarct dementia. SDAT is caused by a complex syndrome of disease processes relating to the chemistry of the brain and, though progressive, is usually gradual in onset and steady in progress. Multi-infarct dementia is caused by narrowed arteries which limit the supply of blood to the brain and so cause localised damage to brain cells. Such damage may be characterised by a major 'stroke' or a series of very minor episodes. There is a tendency to improve after each episode, but if they keep recurring there is steplike deterioration in mental ability.

The early symptoms of dementia affect short-term memory, personal initiative and the quantity and quality of constructive activity. As Lodge describes it, usual hobbies and skills are neglected and conversation becomes stultified, stereotyped and repetitive. Previous personality traits may become exaggerated or may be reversed to quite untypical behaviour, but normal activity in familiar surroundings may be maintained by relying on long-established habits. As the disease progresses, the effects of memory loss become more apparent. The sufferer may be literally 'living in the past' since that is where her remaining long-term memory has taken her and therefore identify those around her with parents or siblings rather than children or grandchildren. She may struggle to escape from a home which has become unfamiliar to go back to the home of her childhood. She may cause havoc by trying to put coal on the electric fire or an electric kettle on the stove. Speech and muscle co-ordination may be affected and finally lower brain functions such as conscious control of the sphincter and bladder muscles and the capacity to swallow. Indeed, as Symonds starkly says:

'Dementia is a dismantling of the human being, starting at the most organised and complex part and proceeding with the failure of the central nervous system components. It involves brain cell death; it progressively involves lower parts of the central nervous system, so that if no other illnesses were to supervene, it would cause death. It follows that dementia is a form of dying. It is an awe-inspiring illness; as those elements have been built up so they are taken apart, and it deserves to some extent the description of second childhood.'[5]

Not all dementing illness will progress in this way, however. If the onset is very late in life, other disease processes are likely to intervene before the deterioration has become serious. If there is not much personality change and the sufferer is able and willing to accept guidance, the effect of the loss of capacity for self-direction may be minimised. If the demented person is also physically disabled, wandering or inappropriate behaviour in the home will not create problems. If surroundings are familiar and habits well-established, as in a couple who have been together for fifty years, one partner may be able to give increasing care to the other over many years until some illness or accident or change in the environment shatters a precarious equilibrium. Other factors, such as sensory impairment and financial circumstances also affect the degree to which the dementia is socially disabling. As Blumenthal says:

'... if one has enough money, one can buy what one needs. One can hire a companion, a cook, and a housekeeper and unless one develops a behaviour problem or mental disability that interferes with one's ability to relate to these people, one will likely get on well. Given enough money, there is not too much difference between a wealthy young lady who does nothing because nothing is required of her, and a demented old lady of means who is equally well cared for. Until the dementia becomes profound, money can compensate for a good deal of functional deficit. One does not have to be able to cook, to dial a phone number, to clean one's house, or to go shopping, if there is no need to do so.'[6]

Thus, although dementia is in itself a progressive organic illness for which there is as yet no treatment, the particular behavioural symptoms shown by the sufferer, the social circumstances and the age of onset can make a great deal of difference to the way in which she can be cared for and the estimates of prevalence quoted above need to be considered in the light of our much more recent knowledge of the varied symptomatology of the illness and the way in which secondary causes of deterioration can be prevented.

The needs of supporters
The myth that adult children are no longer willing to care for their elderly parents has been exploded many times over, though it is still powerful in the public mind. There is ample evidence that relatives *do* care, often at great cost to themselves.[7] But *should* they be

expected to sacrifice the ordinary social pleasures of life, a decent income, a career and an earned pension in exchange for perhaps 20 years of housebound service? And what if there are no relatives? Abrams found from his survey of people over 75 in four urban areas that 35% had no surviving child, and of those who had children nearly 40% said that they lived more than six miles away.[8] Even if there is a close female relative within reasonable reach it is increasingly unlikely that she will be in a position to give constant and intensive care. Sixty-two per cent of women in the age band 25–54 now go out to work compared with 25% in 1951, according to the General Household Survey and the figure would probably be much higher if we had accurate information about part-time and casual employment.[9] The sharp rise in single-parent families and in unemployment means that families will often be dependent on these earnings. Further, the increase in divorce and re-marriage is likely to weaken a sense of responsibility for assorted parents and mean that grandchildren will often grow up without knowing their grandparents, of whom they may have eight or more. In parallel with these changes in social organisation, there is social pressure for equal opportunities for women and abandonment of the assumption that their prime task is to act as unpaid domestic labour. There is, as Finch and Groves point out, no certainty that 'women will continue to accept their cultural designation as carers'—they may 'explicitly reject it, in ideology and in practice, in increasing numbers'.[10] Yet the smallest shift away from the provision of 24-hour care of the very frail in the community will have a dramatic effect on our already grossly over-pressed long-stay hospitals and residential homes. Arie has estimated that a 1% shift into institutional care would require a 25% increase in institutional provision.[11]

It follows that the relatives, neighbours, sheltered-housing wardens and volunteers who are prepared to provide day by day support in the community *must* get the help which they need to enable them to carry on without intolerable strain. Yet what happens in practice? As Bergmann puts it:

> 'Because we run a crisis service, we back failure; we support the people who would be better in institutional care and we neglect those relatives who take on the heaviest burden of care, even though they have the highest prospect of success in keeping the elderly in the community, and in most cases earnestly wish to do so. It is paradoxical that very often those who support the mentally impaired most, and do the best job—the families—get the least help.'[12]

Or, as Dartington says: '... families have to get to the point of a scream of anguish to penetrate the consciousness of those working in the health and social services'.[13]

It is not the 'scream of anguish' but the first whimper of distress which we need to hear. At present, expectations of help are so low that people think that there is no point in asking until they are desperate, and then it is often too late—the carers have had enough.

Planning a 'care package'
As has been indicated in this chapter, the kind of help which may be needed may be a physical treatment, specialist psychiatric help, counselling, the creation of a 'package' of support services or some combination of these. Assessment of what is needed is a skilled task. All too often the response to a cry for help is seen in the professional terms of the person who happens to be on the receiving end. A GP thinks of tests and medication; a home help organiser of 'how many hours a week?'; a community nurse of bathing and incontinence pads, and so on. The members of the relevant professions need to 'think laterally' and to perceive all the dimensions of a situation. This is important with regard to the functional illnesses and acute confusional states, but it is doubly so when a diagnosis of dementia has been confirmed. Here it is certain that progressively increasing support will be needed, ending very probably with 24-hour care, and a care plan is required which takes an accurate and realistic view of current and future needs and plans effectively to meet them. This plan should take account of four main factors:

1. *The actual situation of the person concerned.* How much insight does she have? Does her illness distress her? Is she managing adequately in her own eyes? If so, how far are other people's anxieties realistic and how far are they expressions of exasperation or guilt? What help is really needed and how can this be provided without increasing confusion or causing distress? It is all too easy with dementia sufferers to plan care packages over their heads as if they were inanimate objects. It is true that sometimes their wishes are unrealistic—it is little help if an 80-year old lady persists in affirming that her mother will look after her, or that her daughter (who is in Australia) will pop in. The needs of the supporters have to be considered as well as the wishes of the elderly person herself. Nevertheless, her views should be taken into account even if in the end they have to be disallowed.

2. *Family relationships.* Families are too often unrealistic in their

assumption of responsibility and the help which they accept or reject. One sibling may have been bearing the brunt of support of a parent for years, inwardly resentful of lack of help from the others, and yet refusing help when it is offered. Husbands or wives may be deeply reluctant to expose the symptoms of a loved spouse to strangers, having guarded the secret for so long. Jealousy of the time spent by the care giver at the expense of her own family may intensify marital tensions, and so on. The care package needs to be planned in a way which works through the feelings of those involved and tries to prevent any one person from accepting the entire burden.

3. *Help in understanding the illness.* Supporters need to have the nature of the dementing illness and its effects carefully explained. They need advice on ways in which the ill person can be helped to compensate for loss of short-term memory by making the environment more supportive—a large calendar, a clock, a full-length mirror, written reminders to take medicine or do shopping, gadgets to prevent accidents with cooking, and so on. Simple reality orientation techniques may help (see p. 91). But the emotional needs of the supporters also need to be discussed. Dependency in a hitherto dominant or all-providing parent, wandering, socially distressing behaviour, incontinence, constant repetition of questions, regression to childhood, failure to recognise spouse or children, inability to respond appropriately—any of these possible symptoms of severe dementia will put an intense emotional strain on the carers which must be recognised.

4. *Practical information and support.* There is ample evidence that relatives are very poorly informed about benefits such as the Constant Attendance Allowance to which they are entitled, and they also need to be introduced to the many practical services which *may* be available in the neighbourhood. No two care 'packages' will be identical. A hard-pressed husband may need help with bathing his wife and an anxiety-free evening in the pub once a week. A daughter may be able to cope during the week when her family are at work but desperately need some freedom to give time to them at weekends; a sheltered-housing warden may be willing to cope if her tenant can have a night-sitter on some nights of the week, and so on. The next chapter outlines ways in which these services can be, and in some places are available as part of ordinary statutory or voluntary social service provision and as an essential adjunct to more specialist psychiatric and residential services.

All this implies the availability of someone who has the knowledge, the time and the skill to orchestrate a care plan. Unhappily such paragons are all too rare. GPs, even if they have the interest, are unlikely to have the knowledge or the time. As we shall see in the next chapter, social workers are often untrained in this field, uninterested, or too busy with statutory work; health visitors are frequently reluctant to work with the elderly, although those who have specialised in geriatrics have proved to be invaluable. District nurses are a vital part of the support system, but they cannot be expected to have the time and skill which devising and maintaining a 'care package' demands. Specialist community psychiatric nurses are still relatively rare. If there is a good hospital-based psychogeriatric service, its workers may take on the task, but they may not accept that it is their responsibility to do so. The right answer will not always be the same, but the conclusion seems inescapable that *everywhere* health and social services should come to a clear agreement about responsibility for providing social assessment, casework, and the organising of primary care support for dementing and other chronically ill people, and that the responsible agency should then see that its staff have the time and the training to fulfill this role.

'Need' in institutions
So far this chapter has been mainly concerned with the 'need' of people still living at home. This is primary, because if we cannot offer early diagnosis, treatment and support 'in the community', our institutions will be quite unable to cope with those requiring long-stay care. However, we do need to remember that those who are most severely mentally-disabled are already in long-stay care and their needs and those of their carers are no less pressing. Here too, continuous vigilance is required to ensure that treatable illness does not complicate dementia; that 'caring' does not destroy remaining capacity for self care, decision making and inter-personal relationships; that the rights and needs of carers are considered and respected; in short, that all our available knowledge and skill is used to make the environment as therapeutic as we possibly can. We are not talking only about specialist environments. True, elderly people classified as 'severely mentally infirm' occupy about a fifth of our psychiatric hospital beds, but it has been estimated that for every two severely confused people in psychiatric in-patient care there are a further three in geriatric hospitals (nearly a third of the beds occupied by patients over 65). Also one small survey indicated that 7% of elderly people admitted to acute hospital beds were suffering from dementia and far more are likely to have acute confusional states

arising from their illness and the sudden change of environment or severe anxiety about their ability to cope when they go home.[14] Similarly, as Chapter 8 demonstrates, at least a third of residents in local authority homes have a considerable degree of mental disability, and although there are no figures available, it is reasonable to suspect that private long-stay nursing homes are catering mainly for those who are both physically and mentally disabled. This is only to be expected. Almost any level of chronic physical disability can now be coped with in a domestic setting, providing the person concerned is mentally unimpaired. It is when she does not know what her own needs are and cannot take steps to meet them herself or to summon help that 'constant' as opposed to 'episodic' care becomes unavoidable. As Arie graphically puts it: a paralysed polio victim who can only twitch one eyelid but is of sound mind can call for help when he needs it; he is his own monitor. 'A demented person, on the other hand, far from being her own monitor, is the agent of her own undoing. It is she who leaves the gas on, she who wanders inappropriately in the street, she who neglects to feed herself or keep herself warm, she who persistently disturbs the family or the neighbours to the point that their spirit breaks and they reject her.'[15] Thus, it is inevitable that a rising proportion of elderly people in our long-stay institutions will suffer mental disability and we must face this fact and plan to meet their needs realistically. They have not disappeared because they are no longer being a nuisance to their neighbours or a burden to their family. They are still there and still needing care. Much of this report is concerned with ways in which such care can be more effectively given.

Conclusion

This chapter has attempted to sketch in very broad outline the sort of help needed by elderly mentally-ill people and those who try to help them. Inevitably it makes sobering reading, but this is precisely because a broad outline generalises the problem and there are no generalist solutions. Provision of treatment, support and care needs to be looked at critically and constructively in every relevant service. How does the service we offer affect this client group? How could it be improved? What injection of training, reorganisation or new resources would enable improvement to be achieved? Where does it need to improve integration with other services? These are the questions which need to be painstakingly asked and answered and, as the following chapters seek to show, the answers can be found.

20

REFERENCES
1. Brian Lodge, *Coping with caring: a guide to identifying and supporting an elderly person with dementia.* MIND, London, 1981.
2. Felix Post, Affective illnesses, *in* Tom Arie (ed), *Health care of the elderly.* Croom Helm, London, 1981, 89–103.
3. K Bergmann, Neurosis in old age, *in* Tom Arie, (ed), *Health care of the elderly.* Croom Helm, London, 1981, 104–117.
4. *Dementia in old age.* Office of Health Economics, London, 1979.
5. R L Symonds, Dementia as an experience. *Nursing Times,* 77, 40, 1981, 1708–1710.
6. Monica Blumenthal, Psychosocial factors in reversible and irreversible brain failure. *Journal of Clinical Experimental Gerontology,* 1, 1, 1979, 39–55.
7. See for example Bernard Isaacs and Yvonne Neville, *The measurement of need in old people.* Scottish Health Service Studies No. 34. Scottish Home and Health Department, Edinburgh, 1975.
Bernard Isaacs, Maureen Livingston and Yvonne Neville, *Survival of the unfittest: a study of geriatric patients in Glasgow.* Routledge and Kegan Paul, London, 1972.
Further evidence of the degree to which old people are supported by friends and relatives can be found in Rosamond Gruer, *Needs of the elderly in the Scottish Borders.* Scottish Health Service Studies No. 33. Scottish Home and Health Dept., Edinburgh, 1975.
8. Mark Abrams, *Beyond three-score and ten: a first report on a survey of the elderly.* Age Concern, Mitcham, Surrey, 1978.
9. Olive Stevenson, The frail elderly—a social worker's perspective, *in* Tom Arie (ed), *Health care of the elderly.* Croom Helm, London, 1981, 158–175.
10. Janet Finch and Dulcie Groves, Community care and the family: a case for equal opportunities? *Journal of Social Policy,* 9, 4, October 1980, 487–511.
11. Tom Arie, *Psychogeriatrics: how and why?* Fotheringham Lectures in the University of Toronto, 1979. Unpublished.
12. Klaus Bergmann, How to keep the family supportive. *Geriatric Medicine,* 9, 8, 1979, 53–57.
13. Tim Dartington, *Family care of old people.* Souvenir Press, London, 1980.
14. See ref. 4.
15. See ref. 11.

3 Primary care and treatment services

As the first chapter indicated, the first lines of defence in the treatment and support of mentally-ill elderly people are the basic community services. Most people become ill when they are living in their own homes and it is there that the health and social services need to become aware of their difficulties and offer appropriate help. Specialists may diagnose, treat and advise, but without basic back-up in the community they are useless. Awareness of this fact is growing fast and much innovative work has been done during the last two or three years to improve services which are already there and to add new ones.

This chapter looks at the various aspects of service provision and discusses ways in which it could be improved in quality and range.

General practitioners

If help is needed, the first person to be approached is likely to be the GP. What are the chances of such an appeal being recognised and dealt with adequately? It is, of course, impossible to generalise. Some large practices have a well-informed specialist for their elderly patients; some have attached nurses or social workers who have the time and skill to do a thorough home assessment and talk the problems through with patients and relatives. Some GPs work in relaxed well-staffed practices in pleasant rural or suburban settings, while others are struggling single-handed under massive pressure in our inner cities. Those who have grown up and trained overseas may have had even less experience than British medical students in dealing with the ills of old age and have a cultural and linguistic problem in understanding elderly people and making themselves understood.

Variations of this kind are, however, probably of less importance than personal interest and concern. Some GPs take a strong interest in their elderly patients and some regard them as a lost cause and want as little to do with them as possible. According to one survey report quoted by MIND, only one GP in three is particularly interested in elderly patients or obtains any job satisfaction from this part of his work.[1] Certainly there is widespread evidence that GPs often do not recognise physical illness or 'drug cocktails' which may be exacerbating a dementia or creating an acute confusional state; and they often do not recognise depression, or believe it is the inevitable result of failing health and social isolation or bereavement about which nothing can be done. For example, Gruer's study of a large sample (835) of elderly people in the Scottish Border counties found psychological symptoms in 42%, including some degree of dementia in 8%. In more than half of the sample these symptoms were not recorded by the doctor, although over 40% had seen their doctor in the past 3 months.[2] Harwin studied the mental state of physically impaired elderly people on the caseloads of four district nurses, and found that at least 38% of the sample (48 out of 124) were suffering from a classified psychiatric illness. The mental state of 35 out of these 48 patients was unknown to their GPs and a quarter of the unrecognised patients were assessed by the researchers as ill enough to require psychiatric assessment. Fifteen of the 48 were considered to be suffering from severe dementia.[3]

All this is not surprising since the medical school curriculum too often encourages medical students to despise geriatric medicine and many of the established generation of GPs have trained at hospitals which did not have an established geriatric department. But if basic geriatric training is still woefully lacking, training in psychogeriatrics is still less likely to be offered. The Royal College of Physicians has now stated that 'the Education Committee of the General Medical Council has an obvious responsibility in urging the development of medical school curricula to include the subject' and that advice and instruction on the subject should be made more available during the pre-registration year. The College also urges that the new vocational training programme for GPs should include experience in the special problems of elderly patients with mental impairment and that the subject should be included in continuing education programmes. Policy statements of this kind are one thing, however, and action is another. As the College report itself says, professional training is by its nature conservative and 'the more progressive element in universities and training schools will need the encouragement of public opinion if the appropriate degree of re-orientation of professional training is to be achieved'.[4] We need a concerted effort within the profession and outside it to create awareness of this major gap in basic medical training and to remedy it. However, much can be done to help the present generation of GPs to develop their diagnostic and treatment skills through personal contact with psychogeriatricians and this is a very important function of specialised psychiatric services. Ways in which it can be achieved are discussed in more detail in the next chapter (p. 53).

In general the situation is improving. More young doctors are coming into general practice as their first choice of career and the calibre of recruits to primary care has risen dramatically since 1970. Also compulsory vocational training for general practice should raise standards if there is sufficient opportunity to include place-

ments which give experience in psychogeriatrics during the training
period. However, there is no doubt that there is a long way to go.

Social workers
If an anxious elderly person or her relatives finds that her GP is
uninformed or uninterested, what are her chances of getting a better
response from a social worker? Unfortunately, they may be equally
poor, although there are of course notable exceptions. The BASW
report, *Seebohm across three decades*, quotes research findings
showing that the handicapped and elderly are still rated by social
workers as extremely undesirable clients compared with children
and families, and that only 9% of the clients of experienced social
workers are elderly, compared with 25% of the caseload of untrained
social work assistants. This report comments that research has
shown 'the term of social work assistant to be something of a mis-
nomer, for only rarely did this group of staff carry out tasks on behalf
of social workers, but rather worked on their own cases allocated
on the presumption that the elderly needed services and practical
assistance'.[5] The unpopularity of social work with elderly people is
confirmed by a study of attitudes in a Scottish social work department which found that compared with children, elderly people were
felt to be a poor investment for effort and skill, devalued by society,
too set in their ways to be responsive to social work techniques and
of low priority.[6]

This situation stems in part from history. Until social services were
amalgamated in 1971, following the Seebohm Report, work with the
elderly was the responsibility of Welfare Departments operating
under the 1948 National Assistance Act. This Act gave local authorities power to make arrangements for promoting the welfare of
persons 'who are blind, deaf or dumb, and other persons who are
substantially and permanently handicapped by illness, injury, or
congenital deformity or such other disabilities as may be prescribed
by the Minister'.

This responsibility was carried out by welfare officers who were
often untrained and tended to regard their work with the old in terms
of hygiene and physical safety, rather than encouraging independence and self-determination, though some authorities did have excellent services and trained officers. When the 1959 Mental Health
Act came into force, the community care of elderly people who were
seriously mentally disturbed also became the concern of the newly
created mental welfare departments, and to begin with these were
staffed mainly by ex-mental nurses who had previously been

responsible for carrying out compulsory hospital admissions or social workers (usually untrained) who had been responsible for the supervision of mentally-handicapped people. Gradually, staff with social work training moved into these departments, but their primary interest was naturally in acute mental illness and they often had little knowledge about or interest in old people.

When the two departments were amalgamated with the child care sector and became a unified social services department, staff coming from welfare and mental health tended to be either still without formal social work training or non-graduates who had completed two-year courses in health and welfare, whereas many of the child care officers had degrees as well as professional training. This educational difference, combined with the heavy weight of statutory responsibility in the child care field, influenced the literature produced by social work teachers and encouraged the professional dominance of ex-child care officers in the new departments. The result was that skilled social work tended to be seen in terms of children and families, and the frail elderly, along with the mentally ill, the mentally handicapped and the physically disabled lost out.

There are signs of change, however. The Central Council for Education and Training in Social Work now requires the panels which review the Certificate for Qualification in Social Work (CQSW) course to ask questions about teaching on the elderly, and the content of courses submitted for review does include more concerning ageing than they used to do. The success of Cherry Rowlings' book, *Social work with elderly people*[7] also indicates a new attitude. The need is not so much to put more material about ageing into courses which are already too short and too full for proper professional education, but to make sure that when the basic disciplines are taught, examples concerning ageing are as common as examples from any other field. Thus, as Rowlings points out, the sociology of the family needs to focus on the three or four generation family, rather than the nuclear unit; concepts of role and status need to be explored in relation to the old as well as the young; teaching on human growth and development needs to include the psychology of ageing; and learning and cognition needs to be discussed in relation to old people as well as children. It is admittedly not easy for people who have been teaching for many years to change their approach and sociologists may find it even harder than social work teachers, but it is essential that it should happen.

Another major problem with the CQSW courses is the gap between training and practice. If students find themselves working in Area Teams where work with the elderly is relegated to social work assistants, it is difficult for them to put the teaching they have received into practice and, consequently, difficult for lecturers and tutors to teach the theory with any conviction. One way of breaking out of this vicious circle is the development of new forms of specialist social worker and this is to be welcomed *provided* specialists in old age are seen as educators of their colleagues and sources of requisite knowledge and skills which can be and should also be practised by others. Another new development, to some extent in conflict with this trend towards specialisation, is a growing interest in 'patch' social work—that is mobilising existing and potential community resources and breaking down barriers between professionals and the community by means of very localised service delivery. Clearly this approach can be of great value in constructing and supporting 'care packages' for the elderly, although it raises major questions not only about training and specialisation, but also about decision-making, control, accountability, and relationship to the many services and agencies, both statutory and voluntary whose catchment area is much larger than 'patch' sized. No doubt other models of service delivery will also develop as social work, which is still a very young profession, feels its way forward. But whatever models are chosen, it is essential that they enable social workers to play a much more effective part than they do at present in ensuring skilled assessment and properly planned support for elderly people.

Community-based nursing services
Nurses working in the community have a great deal to offer in identifying early signs of mental stress and offering or mobilising appropriate help, as well as providing physical care. They are often acceptable to elderly people who are suspicious of other service providers; they offer a service which is of clear and practical relevance, and they inherit the respect and confidence built up over many years by the 'district nurse'. However, the various titles and differing roles of nurses now working in the community is somewhat bewildering—and not only to old people. They may be specialists in psychiatric community nursing and the role of these 'CPNs' is discussed fully in Chapter 4. They may be qualified health visitors whose primary task is preventive advice and health education and whose main work is with young families, but who may also have some elderly people on their caseloads or, in rare cases, work entirely with old people. They may be 'geriatric visitors' whose task also is to work in a preventive and educational way with the elderly, but who are not qualified as health visitors. They may be district

nurses (also called community nurses or home nurses) whose primary role is to give physical care and treatment in the home. And any of these may be attached to GP practices, though employed directly by the health service, or may work on a geographical 'patch' basis from health centres and clinics. To make matters still more confusing, no two health authorities operate their community nursing services in exactly the same way. Variations in geography, population density, environment and social history all affect provision.

The value of preventive nursing work with the elderly is well-illustrated by the geriatric visitor service provided within the inner London Borough of Islington. There are now nineteen such visitors employed by the Health Authority who are all trained nurses. Some also have qualifications in psychiatric nursing, ophthalmics and orthopaedics which are invaluable in this kind of work. Eighteen visitors are based in health centres and clinics throughout the District, and one is based in the District General Hospital (DGH) and acts as liaison between the hospital and the community. These geriatric visitors do not give physical care of any kind, since this is the responsibility of the district nurses. Their role is to assess and monitor health, ensure correct use of medication and watch over general well-being. They also teach practical skills in coping with illness and work as health educators and innovators. They accept referrals from any source—clients themselves, relatives, neighbours, district nurses, social services, hospital staff, GPs—even the local greengrocer—and no one is taken off a caseload unless they have moved away or died. Each client is visited at least twice a year regardless of need and those who are socially isolated, very old, have refused supportive services or have a physical or mental disability, receive a much more intensive service. The average caseload is 300, but some visitors carry many more than this.

Regular contact means that a visitor is able to observe not only changes in physical health, but also changes in behaviour which may signal depression or early dementia. It also enables the development of a relationship of trust with clients and their supporters which will encourage them to admit to problems should they occur. The 'patch-based' system of working makes it possible to build up relations with social services, including local home helps, lunch club organisers, meals on wheels distributors and other supporters who can then alert the geriatric visitor if a client is giving cause for anxiety. In addition to their domiciliary work, the visitors run regular groups called 'health circles' on one morning a week in each clinic and centre, and these offer an educational programme on such matters as the care of eyes, ears, teeth, feet, etc., welfare benefits, keeping warm, diet and road safety. The 'circles' have a social as well as an educational purpose; they are a means of encouraging re-socialising after illness or bereavement and encouraging personal pride and independence. One clinic is also offering an experimental screening session in which very basic physical tests are made (with the GP's permission) and the opportunity given for an unhurried talk about symptoms which are causing concern. Unwillingness to 'bother the doctor' is very strong in old people and there is evidence that this facility is of real value. In some areas of the borough, geriatric visitors also attend 'at risk' meetings which are held once a month and are convened jointly by district nurses, the geriatric visitors and social services. Here, clients who are causing anxiety to members of either service are discussed by *all* relevant supporters and a care plan worked out. These meetings are a major factor in reducing confusion over who is responsible for doing what, and ensuring that everyone concerned is working towards the same goals.

Unfortunately, there is not yet any formalised training for this skilled and demanding role. However, Islington does give new geriatric visitors induction and in-service training; very close support is given to new staff during their first year and training days are provided for all staff. After two years' experience of working with the elderly, staff are seconded to take the 15 day Joint Board of Clinical Nursing Studies course No. 940 which offers nurses, who are experienced in the care of the elderly, the opportunity to review their own performance in the light of knowledge gained from professional visits, lectures, seminars and an in-depth study.

It is very difficult to measure the value of a preventive service in terms of reduced hospital admissions or averted crises. Nevertheless, everyone who has contact with the Islington service speaks highly of its value and it seems clear that this is an example which, in one form or another, ought to be much more widely followed.

In areas which are not fortunate enough to have a service of this kind, district nurses can play a valuable preventive as well as curative role. There has been a radical change in the concept of district nursing over the last 5 years or so, and what might be called a 'repair and maintenance' concept of the job—patching up particular injuries and symptoms, bathing, changing etc.—has given way to a 'nursing process' concept in which the nurse is encouraged and in fact required to see her patient not as 'an ulcer' or 'a fractured femur' but as a *person* whose needs must be treated as a whole and for whom the goal is not just the curing of some particular piece of malfunctioning, but the positive promotion of health. District nursing has also changed, in that almost all services now provide some level of 'twilight' (usually 7 pm–midnight) nursing cover and some, but by no means all, provide a night nursing service as well. When a 24 hour service is adequately staffed, this enables a really flexible package of care to be offered. Severely disabled patients can be helped to get up and go to bed; auxiliaries can 'sit in' on a regular basis to give relatives looking after confused people a break during the day or a good night's rest, and nurses can also care for very ill or dying patients who want to stay in their own homes. Again, the job is not an easy one, but at least district nurses now are provided with properly planned courses which, in theory at least, take account of the special skills and awareness required and integrate theory with practice. These nine-month courses are commonly based at polytechnics which may also be training social workers and health visitors and partial integration of their training is proving of great value.

Useful though the contribution of community-based nurses to the welfare of elderly people undoubtedly is, many questions need further study. Boundaries are often blurred between the work of a district nursing auxiliary and that of a home help, for example. Where a home help service is under pressure, nurses may have to provide clients with food or a fire or a clean bed, because there is no one else to do it, while home helps or care aides are increasingly doing the work of nursing auxiliaries (see p. 32). Similarly, district nurses often have to act in an educational or preventive capacity if the health visitors cannot afford the time to look after the elderly and nurses of any kind may find themselves advising on welfare benefits or mobilising community help as if they were social workers. Such role-blurring is greatly to be preferred to an attitude of rigid professionalism, but it can cover up serious deficiencies in service provision and increase the risk of everyone disclaiming responsibility for a particular task.

Another area which needs further study is the now common and officially encouraged practice of attaching both district nurses and health visitors to GP practices. This has many advantages, but it also has potential drawbacks. It can increase travelling time, weaken community links and waste time by duplicating visits to the same place, for example. In addition, health visitors attached to GP practices may find themselves increasingly involved with clinical work and therefore with less time for their special role. Professional isolation and over-subservience to medical direction can also cause problems. A more systematic examination of the advantages and disadvantages of both systems is needed. Also, as Charlotte Kratz has emphasised, we need more systematic investigation of what nurses actually *do* on their visits.[8] The theory is splendid, but domiciliary nursing of any variety is essentially a private affair. Practice has lagged behind theory in the past, and we have no firm evidence that it has caught up. Certainly opportunities for in-service training are not nearly as extensive as they should be: teaching about emotional needs and family relationships in old age is particularly lacking while even basic knowledge about mental illness is still not nearly thorough enough. The community-based nursing services have gone a long way, but its practitioners need to think very hard about where they should be going in the future.

Home helps
The home help service is generally agreed to be the mainstay of community support for the elderly. Its workers provide a visible, practical service, often well beyond their official role or the hours for which they are paid. They get to know their clients far better than a 'hit-and-run' professional can hope to do, and they often become trusted friends. This is of course a rosy view. No service can be perfect and quality certainly varies a good deal from area to area and from worker to worker, but in general home helps deserve their public image. General approval, however, disguises uncertainties and weaknesses in the service's role, status, administration and level of provision. Who qualifies for help? How much, if anything, should clients pay? Should home helps offer only assistance with housework and shopping, or should they give personal care up to a level which could be described as unskilled nursing? How are they best integrated with other personal health and social services? What training should workers and organisers receive? What control should organisers have over their own budget? Why are organisers so seldom promoted to positions of seniority in the social service departments which would enable them to influence policy and future development? These issues are further confused by cuts in local authority spending. The home help service offers a particularly tempting target for cuts because it is labour intensive and its workers are hourly-paid. Cuts can mean that charges are raised, hours per client reduced, and those needing minimum (but very important) help are cut out in order to maintain services for severely disabled people. At the same time, early discharge from hospital and increasing pressure on residential care and the district nursing service result in

home helps being expected to support and give personal care to people with a level of disability which would not have been contemplated a few years ago.

Some authorities have responded to this 'nutcracker' situation by setting up specialist teams paid for by joint funding to take on intensive work (see below). There is, however, no doubt that, given the same scope to work extended hours with one client, and given permission and training to offer personal care, the ordinary home help *can* do a great deal for clients with severe mental and physical disability, provided she has proper supervision and support. For example, an experimental project in Coventry tested the effect of offering an intensive service with selected staff and doubled resources and found that the home helps were able to take over non-skilled personal care tasks which had hitherto been done by nurses and that they developed specialist skills in dealing with the elderly mentally ill and stroke and fracture victims. The study concludes that the extra costs were easily outweighed by savings on admissions to residential care and hospital care and by allowing relatives to continue to work.[9] Another study in Cambridge compared the amount of support provided by domiciliary care assistants to severely disabled clients with that offered by ordinary home helps under the same conditions. It was found that although the home help clients required more nursing support, the two services could provide very similar levels of care, and that there was no need for a separate domiciliary care service[10]. Still more significant is a service run in north Buckinghamshire by a specialist joint-funded home help organiser in association with the Department of Mental Health of the Elderly (DMHE). Here 60 specially-selected home helps, mostly drawn from the ordinary service, are deployed to offer care and support to people referred by the DMHE. They are willing to work early in the morning, during the evening and at weekends as well as during normal hours, and they cope with very severe levels of dementia and other disability. Apart from cleaning up incontinent clients and undertaking all the usual domestic tasks, these home helps get clients ready for day care, settle them back at night, prepare them for relief admissions to short-term care and perform many other personal care tasks. The specialist organiser attends weekly meetings at the DMHE unit to discuss new referrals and current difficulties with the psychiatrist and the community psychiatric nurses, and the Department also offers regular training days for workers. Establishing a service of this kind is not easy. Workers need a telephone so that they can be warned quickly of changes in circumstances and, as they deal with scattered clients over a large district, they also need cars. They must be able to deal with paranoid, depressed and demanding clients, as well as with those who are severely confused and disoriented, and the job demands a strong stomach and a great deal of tact. Personal trustworthiness is even more important than for non-specialist workers, since clients may be unable to give instructions, check change or ensure that the allocated time is actually worked. Also the specialist nature of the job makes it particularly difficult to guarantee minimum hours. If someone who has been given very intensive help goes into hospital, it can leave a gap which cannot quickly be filled with alternative work. But in spite of the problems, the organiser has had no difficulty in recruiting and retaining workers who can cope and who seem to enjoy the demanding nature of the job. It is clear that this specialist team within the ordinary service is supporting people at home who would otherwise have to be in institutional care, though they could not do so without the facilities for day care and relief admission offered by the DMHE. How far this is desirable is another matter. Intensive domiciliary care means that the clients concerned may be considered too disabled for residential care when admission appears unavoidable and the risk of death or injury to a person with severe dementia left on her own all night and for long hours at weekends is undeniably very serious. However, the shortage of long-stay places in Buckinghamshire means that there is little practicable alternative, and this service does prove what *can* be done by ordinary home helps if they are given the proper backing. The service has now been extended to the rest of the county.[11]

It is clear that whether specialist or not, the home help service has a great deal to offer older people with mental disability. It is often acceptable to people who are too suspicious to take any other kind of help; proper assessment of new referrals offers an opportunity for early treatment and creation of a care plan which would otherwise be lost; its workers are in a position to observe and report changes in capacity and circumstances before stress has become critical; and *given proper backing*, they can offer a very intensive and supportive level of care. However, in a time of rising numbers of the very old and acute shortage of residential and long-stay hospital provision, the service is in danger of being burdened with responsibility for intensive care without having the resources or the training to do the job. If home helps are to take their proper place in the gamut of community services, local authorities need to give more careful thought to basic policy in relation to home help provision and its integration with other service providers, and they need to see that domiciliary care is given the status in their social service departments which its importance deserves. At present, untrained social work assistants too often ladle out requests for help to untrained organisers who, in turn, work to administrators who know nothing about the job and who regard home helps as being on a par with any hourly-paid unskilled manual worker (or, being female, rather below par). While this continues to happen we cannot expect the service to realise its potential.[12]

Intensive home care schemes
As was noted above, the traditional home help service is now being augmented in a number of areas by the employment of 'aides' (the actual name varies) who are specifically employed to offer personal care at an intensive level—intensive both in the number of hours per client and in the nature of the care given. The new projects are usually joint-funded by health and social services and they are perceived as a means of enabling early and successful discharge from hospital, preventing or deferring long-term admission to institutional care, providing caring relatives with necessary support and providing terminal care. Although many of the schemes are primarily concerned with the old, they may also be available for younger physically disabled people and for families under particular stress of one kind or another. No two schemes are exactly the same and it is only possible here to cite some examples which illustrate the variety of provision. Details of other projects can be obtained from articles published in the *Health and Social Service Journal* as a result of its admirable 'Joint Care Award' series.[13]

Rochdale was one of the pioneers in this field with a pilot scheme started in 1977. Three home helps were based in the DGH and given responsibility for preparing homes for patients about to be discharged and looking after them for up to 3 hours a day for a month after discharge. The service was not limited to elderly people. After a successful trial, the team was expanded and by June 1981 consisted of two social workers, two organisers, an occupational therapist and twenty-two care workers. They now offer care for an unlimited period and in circumstances in which no return to independence is expected; they will soon be able to accept referrals from out-patient clinics and from consultants on domiciliary assessments as well as from hospital wards.[14]

Another early example is the Crossroads care attendant scheme which was set up in 1977 after ATV, who produce the serial *Crossroads*, helped finance a trial project in Rugby. There are now over 20 similar schemes throughout the country and 12 more steering committees are likely to start providing services within a few months. Each is autonomous, but all conform to a similar structure. Rugby, the prototype, has about 20 families receiving care at any one time from eight care attendants, their work being administered by a part-time organiser. The aim is to provide personal care for very handicapped people. Though assisting people of all ages, they particularly welcome cases where they can help someone who is very handicapped to continue to work. Attendants will stay overnight when relatives are away. They all receive training to nursing auxiliary level, but are not expected to carry out skilled nursing duties. They supplement and complement existing statutory services and work closely with them. They do not set out to provide terminal care or help connected with bereavement problems, but continue to visit if people they have been assisting for some while become very ill. Attendants are paid rates slightly in excess of home help. Costs are met by social service departments, often with joint funding. The Department of Health (DHSS) also helps fund the scheme nationally.[15]

In Oxfordshire, an experimental Home Care Service has been set up to provide an alternative to residential care, support relations and offer intensive short-term rehabilitation. It is managed by a professional team consisting of an organiser, a district nursing sister, a community psychiatric nurse and a social worker, with seven full-time equivalent care assistants. Much emphasis is given to very careful assessment of needs and to 'topping up' other forms of support rather than replacing them. Over half the clients have some psychiatric disability.[16]

As with the specialist home help service described in the previous section, intensive home care schemes are not effective in supporting people with severe dementia who live alone, unless they are backed by day care and relief admission facilities, and even then the person concerned will be at risk at night and at weekends. Home care schemes are, however, of great value in providing help and relief to relatives or others who are already providing extensive support, and they are also valuable in enabling elderly people recovering from a functional mental illness or a severe physical illness to regain their confidence and their ability to cope independently.

Incontinence services
The service which is most valuable when someone becomes incontinent is of course advice and help which will enable continence to be recovered. There is a great deal which can be done to solve the problem by physical investigation and treatment, the use of inconti-

nence charts, regular toiletting routine, ensuring that the lavatory or commode is easily accessible, and so on.[17] As with many other secondary effects of mental and physical disability, it is far too easily assumed that 'nothing can be done' and elderly people and their relatives are often too ashamed or too despairing to ask for help. Williamson, in his study of GPs' knowledge of their patients' disabilities, found that incontinence was one of the most seriously unreported disabling conditions.[18] Proper examination, treatment and advice from GP, community nurse, and if necessary specialist consultant is therefore of primary importance.

For some people, however, treatment and careful management will still not be effective, and the need to launder fouled bed-linen and clothing can be the last straw in looking after a severely disabled relative. There are many pads and garments now on the market which can help with the problem and the Disabled Living Foundation offers detailed information about these.[19] The use of disposable sheets and a waterproof mattress cover also helps a great deal and many authorities now offer an excellent delivery and collection service. However, if patients are severely incontinent of urine, doubly incontinent or very restless, these may not be satisfactory and are, in any case, a long way from being universally available. One alternative is a laundry service which will provide and wash fouled bed linen. For example, Stockport offers two specially-fitted vans to bring foul laundry in sealed bags to the central hospital laundry.[20] A similar, but much smaller scheme, operates in Gloucestershire, specifically for patients referred by the psychogeriatrician and using volunteer transport. In Macclesfield a service has been established which is paid for by joint funding. No doubt there are a number of similar schemes elsewhere which have not been publicised, but there are certainly not nearly enough. It seems unarguable that incontinent laundry services should be a basic facility everywhere.

Night sitters
We know from the work of Sanford[21] that sleep deprivation is one of the prime causes of breakdown in care by relatives of elderly people with dementia. Confusion is often worse at night and many dementia sufferers tend to 'turn night into day' and be most active when everyone else needs to sleep. The sick person may be restless, noisy, incontinent and in danger of falling out of bed, or, if mobile, in danger of falling or causing havoc in other parts of the house. Night sitting services are therefore of great value in enabling caring relatives to relax, knowing that someone else is in charge, and the certainty of getting a good night's sleep on some nights of the week

can enable people to cope during the remainder. Night sitters can also supplement the district nurses in terminal illness or in cases of sudden and severe illness, such as a stroke.

Given the evident usefulness of such a service, it is a pity that its development has been so patchy. A survey carried out in 1975 by Norfolk Social Services Department[22] found that less than half the social service departments in England and Wales provided a service of any description and these varied in size from an average case load of less than one a year to over 450 clients p.a. and budgets (where these were available at all as a separate item) from £110 p.a. to over £200,000. Rates to sitters also varied from 30p an hour to £1.31, and the charge to clients from nothing to £1.10 an hour. The Norfolk report suggested that variations in demand might be related to the amount and effectiveness of publicity about the service and the extent to which it was reaching possible users and the members of relevant professions. Certainly some authorities seem to have hesitated to publicise the service for fear that demand would put too great a strain on the home help service and so reduce daytime provision. Other factors affecting supply and demand include the availability of alternative services provided by the district nurses, the Marie Curie Foundation, or a voluntary body; the availability of suitable sitters; and the rules about eligibility. Some authorities covered by the survey took the view that night care of any kind was the responsibility of the Health Authority and many of them had difficulty in defining a precise line of demarcation between 'night sitting' and 'night nursing'. Indeed, it seems clear that the most successful recent schemes have developed by using joint funding money and providing an integrated night sitting/night nursing service. In Rochdale, for example, the night sitters have been incorporated into the existing 'twilight' and night nursing service, and although they continue to be local authority employees they are supervised and managed by district nursing staff.[23] Obviously, geographical and other factors will influence the most efficient way of providing a service and giving it professional back-up. All sorts of permutations and combinations of home helps, specialist care aides, district nurses and hospital-based staff are possible. However, it is undeniable that no-one can be expected to 'care' for 24 hours a day, and it seems axiomatic that night sitters should be available in one form or another to those who need them.

Voluntary sitting-in schemes
These schemes are quite numerous. The Kent study, *Social care for the terminally-ill at home and the bereaved*, lists eighteen[24], but they

vary greatly in size, intention, and methods of training, payment and recruiting 'sitters'. Some focus on the terminally ill rather than people needing long-term support, some run under the aegis of national organised bodies such as the WRVS and the Red Cross, while others are small, local services inspired by a GP or a local voluntary organisation. In some schemes, although the sponsoring body is voluntary, helpers are paid from client contributions and other sources; in others, they provide their services free.

The most relevant project from the point of view of this report is the 'Day and night sitting service' provided by Plymouth Age Concern. This scheme has been set up to support the statutory domiciliary services and includes day care, night attendance and sleeping-in. Plymouth Age Concern maintains a register of suitable attendants working at a nominal rate on a casual basis whose work is organised by a Welfare Officer, working full-time and accountable to the Director of Plymouth Age Concern. Some of these helpers have nursing qualifications, but this is just a bonus and attendants only offer the care of a good neighbour. The services are used to give caring relatives a regular break (including full weekends) and a night's sleep and to support those who are nervous of sleeping alone after hospital discharge or bereavement, as well as to meet specific individual need. During the year ending 1980, 181 people received 10 438 hours of daytime help; 73 people received 1 118 nights' care and 23 people received 671 nights of 'sleeping-in' support.[25] This well-established project has now been supplemented by a support service specifically intended for the 'mentally frail' living at home. The pilot scheme uses a part-time organiser funded for 2 years by a Trust, and employs attendants with special training who not only relieve relatives but help to rehabilitate clients and encourage them to resume routines of daily living and self care.

Plymouth Age Concern emphasise the value of the specialist organiser's close personal knowledge of the area (she was formerly Plymouth Age Concern's Welfare Officer) and the very careful attention which needs to be paid to assessment of clients' needs, selection and support of attendants, and on-going monitoring. Every client and situation is regularly reviewed. Much time also needs to be spent on consulting with the medical, nursing and social services when the scheme is being set up and gaining the confidence of GPs. Doctors are naturally reluctant to recommend a service which carries such responsibility until they are convinced of its standards and its reliability, and relatives are equally reluctant to give a stranger who has no official designation the run of their home and the care of their dependent relative. Great care, therefore, needs to be devoted to establishing credibility and getting the right kind of referral.

The importance of this was vividly demonstrated by the lack of response to a Sitting-in Service for the Elderly (SISE) based at the Westfield Community Centre, Hinckley. The volunteer organisers did not have sufficient time or financial resources to get the project off the ground and there was also consumer resistance. 'We failed to realise the high degree of reluctance which families caring for an elderly confused relative would have to a stranger entering their home'... "Oh, it's a good idea" a relative would say, "but a sitter would never be able to cope with my Mum", or "I could never allow anyone else in my house to do that". Other factors were professional wariness of using volunteers in this capacity, confusion about their role and difficulty in responding to urgent requests or convincing the GPs.[26]

By contrast, a voluntary body called Search Project, based in Newcastle, has had considerable success with a 'Carers Support Scheme' which uses Inner City Partnership funding to pay a full-time co-ordinator and four part-time care attendants. Several months were spent on establishing good relations with the relevant agencies and statutory services, and especially the home help and community nursing services, and this was followed by intensive training for both co-ordinator and care assistants. This was seen as vital, not only to equip the staff member with necessary skills and knowledge, but also to enable her to pass on useful information to the primary carer. In its first 8 months of active operation (August 1980–April 1981) the project received 128 referrals and offered regular or occasional help to 68 of these. By far the most common sources of referral were the District Nurse (20) and the Social Services Department (17). No case was referred by a GP. The project is now increasing the hours worked from 66 to 80, and is also exploring the recruitment of occasional extra helpers to provide holiday cover for carers. It is likely to develop other services such as a relatives' support group and the provision of practical information. The success of this scheme demonstrates the fruitful alliance which can be developed between statutory and voluntary bodies, the need for 'professionalism' and attention to detail in setting up projects, and the value of very localised service provision.[27]

Boarding-out schemes
An alternative to providing someone to look after an elderly person in her own home is to take her to stay for a shorter or longer time

in someone else's home. These schemes which are variously called 'boarding out', 'fostering', 'family placement', 'home finding', 'supported lodgings' or 'assisted lodgings', are now widely used, though generally on a very small scale in any one place. A detailed research study published in 1980[28] identified 23 schemes caring for 50 people in long-stay placements at the end of April 1980 and 285 clients in 650 short-stay placement weeks in 1979. About half the clients in long-stay placement were mentally ill or mentally handicapped as well as elderly, many having been discharged from long-stay psychiatric hospital wards.

Short-stay placements meet a very wide variety of needs. They relieve relatives (this was the commonest use found in the study) but also offer an alternative to admission to a home if a supporter is ill or on holiday, provide for rehabilitation and recuperation, enable confidence in self care to be recovered after hospital treatment, relieve isolation and so on. The researchers found that most clients were satisfied with the service and several were very enthusiastic. Most of those who had also experienced short stay in residential care preferred the more individual attention provided by assisted lodging. It seems clear that there is considerable scope for spreading and expanding schemes of this kind—especially for the provision of short term care—but they depend for their success on the quality of administration and associated social work. Any attempt to economise on time spent in recruitment of carers, preparation for placement and subsequent back up is likely to be disastrous.

'Bought-in' services
The supplementary services described in this chapter may not meet the particular needs of an individual or may not be available in a particular place. One solution to this problem, which is being tested out in Kent and Gwynedd, is to enable specialist social workers to buy extra help either by using commercially-operated services—for example, taxi transport to a relative's home or meals delivered from a restaurant—or by recruiting a paid helper on an *ad hoc* basis to care for a particular client. Each 'package' is costed, including the unit cost of ordinary social service support such as a home help or meals-on-wheels and the limit allowed (but seldom reached) is two-thirds of the cost of a residential place. The facility is limited to those who would otherwise be candidates for residential care. Although the potential use of commercial services is very wide, in practice the capacity for buying in extra help has been mainly used to recruit locally-based helpers to ensure support when the ordinary

services are not available—particularly the early morning, bedtimes and weekends. The concept sounds simple but these projects do cross a number of boundaries in terms of employment law, financial responsibility, legal liability and so on, and getting them off the ground requires a lot of co-operation from local authority personnel who are concerned in these fields. They also demand skilled, specialist social work, not only in assessing need and matching helper to client but also in continued monitoring of service need and provision. It is no easy option as an alternative to residential care but the experiments do seem to be proving successful in both financial and personal terms.[29]

Voluntary counselling services
As the first chapter of this report has already emphasised, intensity of feeling increases rather than decreases with age. As the time available for change gets shorter, as available choices narrow, as loss and dependency is experienced, it becomes increasingly important to come to terms with the past, to face the future constructively, to sort out relationships which have gone wrong and to learn new ways of adaptation. To do this effectively older people may need to make use of some kind of counselling service through which they can explore perhaps painful thoughts and feelings and come to a realistic perception of present environment and possible future action.

Counsellors may be of any profession; GPs, clergy, social workers and nurses, for example, can and often do offer a counselling service. But although members of any profession can play this role, and those in the 'helping professions' should certainly be offered training to do so, they are frequently too busy or too concerned with other professional aspects of their job, or not temperamentally suited for the counselling task. As a result, a number of organisations have developed specifically to provide counselling services, often using volunteers with professional backing. Many of these deal with particular life experiences or presenting symptoms: examples are the Marriage Guidance Bureaux, the Samaritans and Alcoholics Anonymous. Elderly people may, of course, make use of any of these specialised services which are appropriate to them. However, they may have problems which are not so specific or which are difficult to recognise at first glance. A housing problem may, in fact, be about relationships with relatives or a financial problem about a deep-seated reluctance to apply for a rent rebate, for example. Some organisations are, therefore, attempting to set up agencies which can identify need for counselling help and provide it while, at the same time, coping efficiently with straightforward requests for advice.

Age Concern Scotland has been working in this field since 1974 and has established six services. It is, however, no easy task, demanding as it does long and careful initial planning, very careful recruitment and training of volunteers and long-term professional commitment to their support and to the allocation of cases. Less ambitious projects which are still broadly based may use the services of a skilled and interested professional, such as a clinical psychologist, to offer training to personnel who are already in full-time or extensive contact with elderly people through clubs and drop-in centres or information bureaux. Age Concern Newcastle, for example, has worked closely in this way with a local psychologist. This extension of professional skills by proxy into established voluntary services could be much more widely practised.

Partly because of the difficulties of establishing efficient comprehensive counselling services for the elderly, a number of organisations have chosen to focus on bereavement, which is the most common and potentially dangerous psychological experience of old age. Most people weather this storm, with understanding and help from family and friends, but many would do so with less unhappiness, and perhaps with the avoidance of hurried and mistaken decisions if they had skilled help. Bereavement in old age brings with it more than the loss of a partner. The dead spouse may have shielded the surviving partner by 'acting as a memory', doing the shopping or coping with domestic or business chores. And if the couple have retired to an idyllic cottage in the country or by the sea, the survivor may also find herself in a ghetto of bungalows occupied by widows. Particular problems may occur if there has been a long period of illness before the death so that the partner doing the nursing has been under physical and financial strain, cut off from social contacts and carrying the emotional burden of watching a loved person deteriorate. After such a death, there is a deep sense of deflation, emptiness and emotional vacuum.

The organisation with the greatest experience in this area is Cruse, which was founded in 1959 with the primary intention of supporting widows with dependent children. At the time, it was thought that older people were less in need of help, but it has now been recognised that this is not so and Cruse has extended its activities both to widowers and to older people. The great advantage of Cruse is that it can provide support (simultaneously if this is desirable) at three different levels. It offers group and individual counselling to help members come to terms with their experience of loss; it offers practical advice and assistance; and it offers opportunity for social contact.[30] Although Cruse is by far the largest and best established of organisations working in this field, it is by no means the only one. Some branches of Age Concern are now taking active steps to train and deploy bereavement counsellors. The Family Welfare Association in Hammersmith works with trained volunteers in a project which covers both bereavement and loss. In Camden, the Council of Social Service recruits counsellors who are trained by the Tavistock Institute of Human Relations and who offer help to everyone who registers a death in a particular area. So numerous have these bereavement projects become, in one form or another, that 14 organisations in the London area now meet regularly under the auspices of the London Voluntary Service Council, and it is hoped to set up a loose national federation of bereavement projects in order to make better use of specialist skills and resources.[31]

Relatives' support groups
It is of key importance that the relatives and other supporters of chronically mentally ill elderly people should have opportunities of seeking advice, sharing their feelings and communicating with professional staff. An increasingly common way of achieving these ends is through the use of relatives' groups. These take many different forms. They may be directed towards the relatives of people still living at home, or towards the relatives of people attending a particular day hospital or centre, or towards the relatives of people already in long-term care (see p. 95). They may be primarily concerned with providing practical information and advice on services and management or they may have their main emphasis on sharing the emotional distress and alleviating the sense of shame and isolation which caring for a demented relative can bring. They may be used as an opportunity to improve staff/relative contact and co-operation in 'sharing the caring' or they may provide the basis for pressure group activity to get services improved and raise public awareness of the problems.

Most of these groups, so far, have come about through the initiative of concerned professionals and offer a service to relatives who are already known to a psychiatric service. However, there is also a small but growing attempt to establish 'self-help' mutual support and pressure groups in the community. Examples are Support the Elderly Mentally Infirm (SEMI) in Bristol and Age Concern in Birmingham.[32] MIND has published a leaflet giving advice and information on setting up such groups[33] and encourages its local branches to initiate projects of this kind. On a national basis, one encouraging development is the formation of the Alzheimer's Disease Society (which also covers related dementia illnesses). The Society aims to promote local branches, starting with a nucleus of two or three families of sufferers, friends, doctors and other workers in the health service 'as well as anyone interested in promoting the welfare of the Society on payment of the membership fee'. Through these local branches and also through literature and publicity, it tries to support families who are coping with the disease, disseminate knowledge of the aids and services available and see that nursing care is provided during the last stages. The Society also seeks to promote research and the education of the general public in understanding the nature of the illness through the press, media and fund-raising.[34]

Conclusion
This brief review of community services has covered a great deal of ground in a way which is necessarily cursory and inadequate. However, it does demonstrate a number of points. First is the need for greatly improved training of GPs, community nurses and social workers in the psychiatric and emotional problems of older people. These three services between them provide the community's safety net, and if those who work in them are unable or unwilling to pick up the 'whimper of anguish' before it has become a scream and take appropriate action, no one else is likely to do so. Second, there is the need to deploy the home help services so that referral for help is used as a means of screening people at risk and ensuring that home helps are used in the most effective possible way. This involves careful integration of the home help services with other social service and health care provision, and with the help provided by family and friends; it carries implications for training and status of both workers and organisers and means that domiciliary care must be represented at a senior level of social services planning. An *ad hoc* attitude to the home help service is no longer good enough. Third, there is the need for flexible voluntary and statutory back-up services which can offer relief to relatives and fill the gaps in the 'care package'. There is ample evidence that these services can be made to work effectively and at relatively low cost given really careful preparation and continued support from the relevant professionals. They can make all the difference between success and failure in 'community care' and they need to become the rule rather than the exception. Finally, there is the need to maintain a constant awareness of the 'feelings' needs of older people and their relatives, and to ensure that means are available to work through them constructively by means of counselling services, relatives' groups and the provision of opportunities for training in counselling for interested professionals and

volunteers. None of this is 'pie-in-the-sky'; all the services described have been proved to work somewhere. What we need now is to make sure that they all work everywhere.

REFERENCES
1. MIND, *Mental health of elderly people—MIND's response to the DHSS discussion paper 'A happier old age'*. MIND, London, 1979.
2. R Gruer, *Needs of the elderly in the Scottish Borders*. Scottish Home and Health Department, Edinburgh, 1975.
3. B Harwin, Psychiatric morbidity among the physically impaired elderly in the community: a preliminary report, *in* J K Wing and H Hafner (eds), *Roots of evaluation*, Oxford University Press for Nuffield Provincial Hospitals Trust, Oxford, 1973.
4. Organic mental impairment in the elderly: implications for research, education and the provision of services: a report of the Royal College of Physicians Committee on Geriatrics. *Journal of the Royal College of Physicians of London,* 15, 3, July 1981.
5. J Cypher (ed), *Seebohm across three decades*. British Association of Social Workers, Birmingham, 1979.
6. N Nicholson and J Paley, What are the principles of practice? *Community Care,* 371, July 30 1981, 19–20.
7. Cherry Rowlings, *Social work with elderly people*. George Allen and Unwin, London, 1981.
8. Charlotte R Kratz, *Care of the long-term sick in the community*. Churchill Livingstone, Edinburgh, 1978.
9. S Latto, Help begins at home. *Community Care,* 312–313, April 24 and June 12 1980, 15–16, 20–21.
10. K R Simons and R W Warburton, *A sensible service*. Social Services Department, Cambridgeshire County Council, Cambridge, 1980.
11. Further information from the Area Social Services Department, George Street, Aylesbury, Bucks.
12. Rodney Hedley and Alison Norman, *Home help; key issues in service provision*, Centre for Policy on Ageing, London, 1982. (CPA Reports 1).
13. See, for example, N Millard, The seeds of support are sown and the harvest is strength. *Health and Social Service Journal,* 89, 4665, October 26 1979, 1390–1 (Barnet).
R Lovelock, Caring at home. *Health and Social Service Journal,* 91, 4757, July 31 1981, 925–927 (Hampshire).
M Dexter, Intensive care at home. *Health and Social Service Journal,* 91, 4730, February 13, 1981, 170–172 (Avon).
Also *Report on the first twelve months of the pilot community support scheme for the elderly*, Surrey County Council, December 1979.
N Dunnachie, Intensive domiciliary care of the elderly in Hove. *Social Work Service,* 21, November 1979, 1–3 (East Sussex).
Further information on innovative services can also be obtained from E Ferlie, *Directory of initiatives in the community care of the elderly*. University of Kent, Personal Social Services Research Unit, Canterbury, 1980.

14. Michael Scofield and Lyndon Price, Helping hands at home. *Health and Social Service Journal*, 91, 4749, June 26 1981, 766–769.

15. Kay Wells, *Social care for the terminally ill at home and the bereaved: report to the Kent County Council Social Services Committee*. Kent Voluntary Services Council, 1980.

16. K Quelch, A choice to stay at home. *Health and Social Service Journal,* 91, 4770, October 29 1981, 1336–1338.

17. B Browne, *Management for continence*. Age Concern England, Mitcham, 1978.

18. J Williamson, Screening, surveillance and case-finding, *in* Tom Arie (ed) *Health care of the elderly: essays in old age medicine, psychiatry and services.* Croom Helm, London, 1980.

19. Disabled Living Foundation, 380/384 Harrow Road, London W9 2HU.

20. P. Turton, Clean sheets. *Nursing Times* (*Community Outlook*), 74, 36, September 8 1977, 41–46.

21. J R A Sanford, Tolerance of debility in elderly dependents by supporters at home: its significance for hospital practice. *British Medical Journal*, August 23 1981, 471–473.

22. Norfolk Social Services Department, Research Training and Personnel Division, *Night sitting services: research report and summary*. Norfolk Social Services Department, Norwich, 1975.

23. (No author) '. . . and at home'. *Health and Social Service Journal*, 91, 4752, July 17, 1981, 861.

24. See ref. 15.

25. *1980 Annual Report*, Age Concern Plymouth, Elspeth Sitters House, Hoegate Street, Plymouth, 1980.

26. K Lowles, *Community care of the confused elderly: experience of group work undertaken in the Hinckley area of Leicester*, Westfield Community Centre, Rosemary Way, Hinckley, May 1981.

27. *Carers support scheme annual report*, 221 Woodstock Road, Scotswood, Newcastle-upon-Tyne.

28. Patricia Thornton and Jeanette Moore, *The placement of elderly people in private households: an analysis of current provision*. University of Leeds, Dept of Social Policy and Administration, Leeds, 1980.

29. David Challis and Bleddyn Davies, A new approach to community care for the elderly. *British Journal of Social Work*, 10, 1, Spring 1980, 1–32.

30. Further information from Cruse House, 126 Sheen Road, Richmond, Surrey.

31. Further information from the London Voluntary Service Council, 68 Chalton Street, London W1.

32. Further information from Support the Elderly Mentally Infirm, Bristol Council for Voluntary Service, 9 Elmdale Road, Bristol and Age Concern Birmingham, Carr's Lane Church, Carr's Lane, Birmingham.

33. MIND, *Who cares about relatives?: support groups for relatives of elderly people who are mentally ill*. MIND, London, 1979.

34. Further information from C G Brousson, Development Officer, Alzheimer's Disease Society, 158/160 Balham High Road, London SW12 9BN.

4 The role of specialist psychogeriatric services

The first two chapters of this report emphasised the importance of early recognition of symptoms of mental illness in elderly people and the easy availability of skilled diagnosis and treatment. Diagnosis is no easy task. As we have seen, inappropriate medication and sudden changes in social circumstances can produce acute confusional states which are easily mistaken for dementia or may be superimposed on dementia, and serious depressive illness is also easy to mistake for dementia. Family relationships, personality, previous psychiatric history and a host of other factors can complicate both diagnosis and the care or treatment plan. Once made, the plan may need skilled orchestration of hospital and community-based resources to enable it to be carried out. It is thus not surprising that the demands of this work have resulted during the 1970s in the rapid growth of specialist psychogeriatric services run by teams of skilled and concerned professionals who all contribute to the assessment and treatment process. The consultant psychogeriatrician fights for resources and shapes the overall 'philosophy' of service provision and he carries ultimate responsibility for it, but without the rest of the team he can do little. Nurses working in hospital wards, day hospitals or the community, occupational therapists and their aides, social workers and psychologists, all have a vital role to play in creating a system which is efficient in diagnosis, therapeutic in treatment and supportive in on-going caring. This chapter looks briefly at the role which the members of these specialised teams can play and at some of the dilemmas which they face, but it must be remembered that the fieldwork done for this report inevitably focused on 'centres of excellence'. It shows what *can* be achieved rather than what is now being generally achieved. Even in this limited area it has not been possible to visit more than a few of the hospitals which are known for innovative or excellent service. The examples cited of variations in 'philosophy' and technique are therefore only meant to be illustrative. There are many others which could have been visited and used as sources of information if time had allowed.

'Psychogeriatricians'

At the beginning of the 1970s, there were just over a dozen psychiatrists in Britain who might have described themselves as 'psychogeriatricians' and there were less than half a dozen special district services for mentally ill old people. In 1980 a national survey identified 106 consultant psychiatrists providing special psychiatric services for the elderly, of which 39 were full-time and 52 more than half-time. Not all those practising were identified, however, and the actual number is about 120.[1] It is now official NHS policy to provide at least one such consultant in each health district, and there is strong pressure to give the subspeciality formal status. Such overall figures, encouraging though they are, disguise enormous local variations: 87 districts have a specialised service, but some 110 do not. Scotland and south-east England are much better served than the midlands and the north. Moreover, providing a post and making an appointment does not guarantee a high quality of service. Well-trained people are in desperately short supply and competition for posts is not high since the speciality is not popular. (A DHSS survey from March 1975 to February 1976 found that there were 7·2 applicants for each consultancy in general psychiatry, but only 3·8 for each psychogeriatric post.) Moreover, some of the applicants may be more interested in getting a job than in the specialism for its own sake, and as one observer has trenchantly observed, 'To have failed to gain a consultant post in general psychiatry does not make one a better candidate for psychogeriatrics'. Even if the person appointed is able and interested, he cannot provide a reasonable service unless he is given the resources he needs and the understanding and support of his colleagues in psychiatry and geriatrics. The question of what resources are needed to provide a viable service is discussed in more detail below.

Assessment procedures
It should not be assumed that the patient needs to be admitted for assessment. Some psychiatrists lay great stress on the value of examining new referrals in their own homes where it is possible to assess functioning in a familiar setting and pick up clues relating to history, previous standards, deterioration, etc. at first hand, as well as making the friendly informal contact with the carers which is essential to future maintenance. For example, Colin Godber at Moorgreen Hospital, Southampton believes that an experienced doctor, after a detailed domiciliary visit of this kind, can make a provisional diagnosis and draw up a treatment plan which may have no reference to hospital admission or outpatient treatment. Such a plan might include advice to the GP regarding medication; follow-up by the psychiatric community nurse and arrangements for relief care at a local day centre. It is hard to judge how far this approach is making a virtue out of necessity, since Godber has no day hospital available for assessment purposes and no easy access to facilities for physical tests. Certainly such a service relies heavily on the willingness of himself and his colleagues to spend much of their time in domiciliary work (they reckon to meet all requests within 24 hours) and on the availability of a team of specialist com-

munity nurses to follow up, mobilise community support and maintain contact, so that if the situation changes or the initial assessment proves incorrect, swift action can be taken.

By contrast, the Brighton Clinic in Newcastle is based in the district general hospital (DGH) and has a well-equipped and staffed day hospital as well as assessment beds and easy access to the whole gamut of physical examinations. Here, the consultant, Gary Blessed, does not carry out home assessment visits himself, but his Senior Registrar is willing to respond to requests both from GPs and from the local social services area teams. If further investigation is needed it is carried out, if possible, on a day patient basis using the full range of professional skills including those of an occupational therapist, physiotherapist and psychologist as well as nursing staff and trainee psychiatrists. Usually information about the home background is provided by the clinic social worker or by a field social worker who already knows the patient, or it may be provided by relatives in an interview at the clinic.

R A Robinson, formerly at the Royal Victoria Hospital, Edinburgh, offered an on-call domiciliary visit as a screening measure, but unless the situation called for urgent admission, followed this up with more thorough investigation at his out-patient clinic. He said that this double measure may seem uneconomic and unnecessary, but 'the sequence enables the home visit to be brief' and 'we believe that the frequency with which investigations have shown unsuspected or complicating medical features justifies this policy of seeing all referrals at great depth'.[2]

At the Bevendean Hospital, Brighton, Tony Whitehead puts primary emphasis on using the day hospital for assessment and for long-term support, and he only admits patients if there are strong social grounds such as acute family tension or intolerable behaviour. He believes that leaving home by day is an ingrained social habit and, therefore, not disruptive of confidence and orientation so that assessment is easier than in a ward. By contrast, Ian Thomson, at Whitecroft Hospital on the Isle of Wight believes that assessment and treatment can be productively combined when the person concerned is under constant observation and that behaviour at night is of crucial importance; also that a period away from usual habits and relationships, and in company with younger people, can in itself be beneficial and so affect the long-term treatment plan. Wherever it takes place, assessment will include careful physical examination, tests of memory, mood, orientation, etc., analysis of self-care abilities and a description of the social situation and support network, as well as a detailed history. The checklist used by the Moorgreen doctors on their domiciliary visits is printed as Appendix 1 since it gives a useful outline of the ground which has to be covered. Assessment is, of course, a continuing procedure, but it is essential that at any particular time, both the psychogeriatric team and the community supporters should be clear about what they are trying to do, how they are trying to do it and who is responsible for getting it done. It is only too easy to assume the problem has been solved by defining it and then forgetting about it, or taking some kind of 'non-action' such as putting a patient on a waiting list.

Treatment

Treatment may take many forms. Sometimes the first step is simply to take the patient off all drugs and monitor the effect. Physical mobilisation, retraining in self-care, improved diet and providing relief from loneliness or family tensions can all have their effect. Involving relatives and other supporters in discussing the nature of the illness and future care plans is a very important aspect of treatment. Thus, while more obviously medical interventions such as anti-depressant or sedative drugs, electro-convulsive therapy and treatment of physical illness do play their part, treatment in a psychogeriatric unit is by no means the sole province of doctors.

This report is about the provision of services rather than the details of diagnostic or therapeutic techniques, but it is worth emphasising the extent to which various forms of psychotherapeutic and behavioural therapy are now being used in the treatment of elderly people. At St James' Hospital, Portsmouth, for example, a regular weekly group is run for the functionally ill. Patients are selected on the basis of having no serious sensory difficulties, their ability to verbalise and their diagnosis. Topics which come up include marital difficulties, moving house, dependence/independence issues, and gaining insight into attention-seeking or demanding behaviour and guilt feelings. The hospital also runs a regular small out-patients group which meets weekly over an 8-week period and is particularly focused on adjusting to reality and accepting the loss of home, status, health, family relationships or financial security. Patients selected for this are usually lonely, often rebelling against ageing, finding retirement stressful or having difficulty in coming to terms with physical disability and loss of independence. Such psychotherapeutic groups appear to be rather more authority-oriented than would be usual with younger patients and the therapists make deliberate use of the dependency relationship to encourage movement towards independence: 'the doctor says I must try. . .'. They are also more protective of existing defence mechanisms since interpretations which might threaten a life-time of learned behaviour could destroy existing patterns of adaptation without the time being available to rebuild more constructive alternatives. They therefore contain a strong supportive element, building up confidence in ability to cope and gently shifting perspectives.

Another example is at Moorgreen Hospital, Southampton, where all the 25 patients on the acute assessment ward are encouraged to attend a weekly ward meeting which works on traditional non-directive group therapy lines—the therapist throwing back requests for authoritative comment to the patients, and patients and staff tolerating long silences with apparently little tension. There are problems with deafness and inappropriate reminiscence and repetition, but deep feelings and fears are also often expressed, and the group has proved to be particularly valuable for those with severe depression who are being treated with drugs or ECT. The same therapist does marital work with elderly patients, using a co-therapist in a 2 : 2 relationship and also runs an out-patient group not only for ex-patients but also for new referrals if this is thought to be the most appropriate form of treatment.

The examples cited above rely almost completely on verbal interaction to provide a vehicle for feeling, but some therapists believe that this is too threatening to elderly people who may be totally unused to discussing feelings and who may have been brought up to believe that one should not express emotion in public. For such people, it may be helpful to provide a reassuring external focus for discussion. At the Royal Victoria Hospital, Edinburgh, for example, occupational therapists and nurses use a few lines of evocative poetry to trigger discussion of deeper feelings or invite a patient to bring some treasured possession and talk round it. Music is also used to encourage discussion of feelings, such as relaxation, grief, struggle with the elements, old joys of dancing and singing, etc. In an art group, patients are invited to paint on a theme such as success and failure or sadness and happiness, and then put their picture up and explain what they were trying to express. These 'feelings' groups are closely associated with others intended to increase confidence and modify behaviour in practical ways (see p. 51).

Another therapeutic technique which has aroused considerable debate about its utility, and indeed its ethics, is 'classroom reality orientation' (RO). In its simplest form, this technique involves taking a small group of patients with memory loss into a separate room and going through routines designed to reinforce their aware-ness by encouraging them to name themselves, the place, the date, etc., and to take part in very simple activities such as naming objects, counting, letter recognition and spelling. Much encouragement and praise is offered. The objective, as Woods and Holden describe it, is to help the person succeed, to know what is happening and to communicate.[3] Critics of this technique say that it demeans elderly people by treating them as young children and that in unskilled hands it can become rigid, bullying and psychologically destructive. Evidence is also thin as to the beneficial effect in functional and behavioural terms, as opposed to purely cognitive improvement such as increased scores on information and orientation tests. More basic still is the problem of deciding when the point has been reached at which pressing people who have lost almost all their capacity for short-term memory becomes cruelty rather than kind-ness. *Why* should they have to remember? What useful purpose does it serve? This is a question which always needs to be asked and answered both in terms of practical happiness and in terms of under-lying residual ability. It certainly seems that one of the problems with 'classroom RO' is that it is too often used without clear goals or with patients who have little hope of benefiting.

The use of classroom RO is too often confined to patients with very severe memory loss when it could be most useful for depressed patients with symptoms which may be mistaken for early dementia, as well as patients who have depression *and* early dementia. For example, Woods and Holden describe how:

'Mrs B sat in her chair for some months, declaring that she was incapable of doing anything. She felt that she was useless, a nuisance and frequently wept with despair. She believed that she would not do anything right in RO, but once there, she found that she could do things she had thought impossible. She required a great deal of reassurance and encouragement, but smiles began to appear as success after success occurred. Her self care improved, and she was well enough to be discharged within a few weeks.'

One technique which is frequently used in RO groups, but which is now gaining attention in its own right, is the use of 'reminiscence therapy'. The capacity of elderly people to remember the distant past is utilised to increase their sense of identity, their orientation and their recognition of each other as individuals. Reminiscence of this kind may be very simply focused on an anniversary (the day the Second World War broke out, or the Queen's Coronation, for example), or it may be focused on old postcards and snaps, or on personal possessions. The Education Department of Help the Aged has now produced a guide to the use of this technique and a series of tapes and slides designed to evoke memories.[4]

Therapeutic techniques of the kind described above may be combined with formal or informal behaviour therapy. For example, someone who has lost confidence in her ability to live independently might be gradually taken through a 'hierarchy' of carefully graded activities till she reaches a planned level of achievement. Much group work can also be geared towards recovering confidence and sharing anxieties. At the day hospital of the Royal Victoria Hospital in Edinburgh, for example, treatment may include role plays in which anxiety-making situations are acted out and appropriate behaviour discussed, and selected patients go together on outings which involve sharing transport, restaurant and lavatory facilities with the general public.

It will be evident from these examples that carrying out treatment in the acute wards of a pyschogeriatric hospital or in a day hospital can be an interesting and demanding task which requires as much or more skill as working with younger patients. This fact needs to be more fully brought home to members of the relevant professions who too often believe that work in a psychogeriatric unit is a dull and depressing business which will not enable them to use their skills to the full. It also needs to be brought home to the general public who too often see referral to a psychogeriatrician as 'the end of the road', as well as a social disgrace.

Hospital-based social workers
It will be evident that hospital-based social workers have an important part to play in the assessment and treatment process and still more so in liaising with the community-based services to ensure adequate support after assessment and discharge. Unfortunately their anomalous position all too frequently makes it difficult or impossible for them to fill this role adequately. Until 1974 medical social workers were a separate branch of the profession with their own recognised training and qualifications and they were recruited and employed by the NHS. In 1974, however, the Central Council for Education and Training in Social Work (CCETSW) took over the training role and hospital social workers became part of social services department staff, paid from the social services budget, but offering no clearly visible benefit to the rest of the department. They

may, in fact, be seen as an extra burden since it is their job to identify need in hospital patients and make appropriate referrals. If they are not there, the referral may never be made. These posts thus offer a very tempting target in hard financial times. If this is true of all medical social work, it is doubly true of appointments in psychogeriatric units, since, as we have seen, social service departments give low priority to social work with the elderly.

This has been well illustrated by Lynne Jacobs, in her descriptive study of eight leading psychogeriatric services carried out in 1980.[5] She found only one (at the Withington Hospital in Manchester) where there was 'an actual social work team involved in psychogeriatrics' and this had only been achieved by the team leader 'continually putting forward to the social services department the need for a professional approach to this type of work and the need for a very comprehensive social work service'. In Southampton Colin Godber had only one social worker for two days a week (though he now has a second, full time one). In Tower Hamlets, at the time of Jacobs' visit to the London Hospital, 'social work support to the psychogeriatric services was practically non-existent' and the services based on Tindal Hospital in Aylesbury were about to be entirely without social work support as the one part-time worker was about to leave, and there was considerable doubt about whether she would be replaced. Even in the Health Care of the Elderly unit in Nottingham—a unique teaching unit which combines geriatric, orthopaedic and psychogeriatric treatment—the local authority had chosen to freeze the geriatric social work appointment and leave the social worker in the psychiatric unit coping with both departments. If these deficiencies arise in some of the best units in the country, what, one wonders, happens elsewhere?

What role should a social worker specialising in psychogeriatrics play if she *is* there to play it? In the first place, she has a vital educational responsibility. She is not there to take over from the field social workers, but to work with them and with the primary care teams, community psychiatric nurses and residential care staff to develop deeper understanding of the needs of mentally ill elderly people and ways in which they can be treated and supported. She also should play a directly therapeutic role in family and marital therapy and personal counselling, and in running relatives' groups and in-patient and out-patient groups. And all this, in addition to the more bread-and-butter aspects of hospital social work—co-ordinating discharge arrangements, advising on benefits and finding residential placements, for example. In practice, however, the extent to which her role is understood either by colleagues in the hospital or in the area teams is very variable. At worst, she can be a scape-goat, blamed by hospital staff for the inadequacy of community resources and delay in obtaining them, overloaded by area teams with work which they have no time for, and torn between awareness of neglect of her discharged patients and the impossibility of following them up herself. At best she is part of the team, both within the hospital and within the community, providing a vital channel for communication between them.

The educational role of the psychogeriatric team

Not only the social worker but the whole hospital team has a vital part to play in educating, supporting and advising primary carers. This demands time, effort and a clear, positive commitment to the value of the work. A domiciliary visit done *with* the referring agent can be a valuable educational process (even though pressure of time may make it difficult to set up). Much can be learned through case discussions and what Peter Jefferys calls 'indirect consultation'. By this he means giving advice on further action or management without actually seeing the patient—'an extension of the already extensive "indirect consultative service" which many of us in hospital practice already conduct over the lunch table with colleagues'. Jefferys believes that the 'psychiatrist needs to take the initiative to try and meet and speak to as many as possible of the 100 or more GPs practising in his district and, as a minimum, give them clear advice on the facilities available in the specialist service, on its strategy and mode of access to the service'. He also suggests that in a large group practice or health centre serving more than 15 000 people, it may be productive for the psychiatrist or a member of his team to join regular seminars/case conferences. It is not only GPs and social service departments which need to understand the structure of the specialist service and know how and when to use it. But such information must be two-way. As Jefferys says:

'At a personal level the psychiatrist and the specialist team must make the effort to learn about the available services, to meet key personnel and convey appreciation for those services which are provided as well as grumble at those that are not. . .'

Jefferys spends one session a week leading regular seminars with mixed educative/management support functions in area social work offices, day centres and residential homes. He finds this well worth while, not only in improving knowledge and care in the community and offering opportunities for 'indirect consultation' but also in enabling him to make better judgements about the skills and limitations of individual social workers and residential homes which are valuable in planning support and care for individual patients.[6] It is commitment of this nature and this level of intensity on the part of the psychogeriatric team which enables the community to care.

Relatives' groups

Education and support of a rather different kind is provided when the psychogeriatric team take responsibility for running relatives' groups. As we have already seen, such groups offer an invaluable opportunity for the relatives of patients, and especially of patients with dementia, to share their experiences, offer each other practical support and press for improvement of services. When they are initiated and run by the psychogeriatric team, they also provide a convenient opportunity to keep informed about the home situation and to offer practical advice on management, as well as emotional support. This is how a relative describes her experience of attending a group at St James' Hospital, Portsmouth.[7]

'It is common experience that most relatives tend to feel cut off from friends and neighbours because of the very nature of the mental deterioration from which the patients are suffering; their difficulties are so varied and so unusual that they keep most of them to themselves. The mere fact of being among folk to whom these difficulties are commonplace often brings about a rapid and remarkable return of confidence. "I found I was not alone" is repeatedly heard. . . .Over the first year we heard stories of violence and foul language (quite out of character) directed by the patient at the relative. We heard of loss of understanding by a patient of a husband/wife partnership which had existed for decades. We heard of eccentric behaviour seemingly adopted by a patient merely to annoy the relative and render domestic tasks more difficult. We heard of "lucid intervals" when an old relationship seemed about to be re-established. Stories of a struggle to combat incontinence were common, and many spoke of efforts to maintain the patient's interest in what had been his normal pursuits. It impressed tremendously that relatives continued the care and custody of the patient until in danger of nervous collapse.'

Practical difficulties are often encountered in running such groups. If the assessment ward is based in a psychiatric hospital, this is likely to be geographically isolated and attendance correspondingly difficult. If the group is attached to a day hospital, relatives of patients who are not due to attend on that day may be unable to leave them. If the meeting is held in the evening to enable working relatives to attend, there may be difficulties in finding a 'granny sitter'. When groups include relatives of both depressives and dementia sufferers, the difficulties experienced by different members of the group may vary widely, so that sharing is difficult. To some degree the difficulties and emotional problems of spouses will differ from those of a younger generation and some people, particularly the elderly, feel anxious or threatened in a group setting and are unable to use it to verbalise their problems.

Leadership may also present problems. It is important to prevent the group from turning into a question-and-answer session at which relatives demand 'black and white' responses from 'experts'. It is also important that they should not become 'moaning sessions' at which nothing is done but grumble about the lack of facilities or the hardness of fate or the price of electricity. On the other hand, too heavy a focus on 'feelings' can also be threatening and groups need to move between emotions and practicalities. It always needs to be remembered that the prime aim is *supportive* and there may be dangers in making members too aware of the ambivalence of past family relationships or of maladaptive patterns of behaviour which are now too entrenched for change. As one charge nurse put it, 'We can't afford to knock them down and build them up again'. But, although running successful relatives' groups requires both skill and effort, there is no doubt that they do offer an immensely valuable opportunity for relieving the sense of isolation and of unique pain and loss which is such a common feature in the strain of caring for mentally-disabled elderly relatives and the opportunity of joining such groups should be open to everyone in this situation.

Management issues

There are a number of complex issues to be taken into account when considering where mentally-ill elderly people should be treated. Should the functionally-ill be segregated from the organically ill? Should the old be segregated from younger patients? Should they be treated in a modern district general hospital with access to other specialities and to sophisticated diagnostic facilities, or in a setting where it is easier to create a relaxed and non-clinical environment? The possible variations are endless. Many services are still based in the old mental hospitals which are often very isolated geographically, making visiting arduous and tending to cut the service off from the community, while also carrying a still frightening stigma for elderly people who recognise it as 'the lunatic asylum'. Huge rooms and long corridors make it difficult to encourage a homely atmosphere, and ward staff may prefer to work with younger patients. It may also be difficult and time consuming to carry out the physical tests needed for thorough assessment of elderly patients. On the other hand, it is likely that the long-stay and assessment beds will be on the same site, making supervision and relief admission easier (see p. 90). Dedication and imagination on the part of consultants and their teams *can* overcome the problems, but it needs very positive and continuing effort to do so.

Placing a psychogeriatric service in a geriatric hospital, carries a different range of advantages and drawbacks. Isolation may still be a drawback of course, and old-fashioned buildings and lack of easy access to diagnostic and physical treatment facilities are again likely to create problems. On the other hand, the stigma of admission will be related to age rather than insanity and an easy and co-operative working relationship should (but by no means always does) exist between the two specialities. The two consultants may run their admission and discharge policies at a different tempo. For example, one may be determined to keep beds available for relatively rapid and easy admission for assessment and treatment, but operate a ruthless discharge policy and set very strict limits on long-term provision; the other may be less ruthless but acquire silted-up wards and so have lengthy waiting lists for urgent treatment. In that situation, GPs trying to get help for a patient with physical *and* mental disabilities will plump for the consultant whom he thinks will admit quickly, and this can put an unfair strain on the service concerned. There may also be different management styles in the two teams, which can give rise to misunderstanding and misconceptions especially between nursing staff. These may be heightened if one nursing officer is responsible for all staff and she is not psychiatrically trained. Another danger is that psychiatric staff may feel themselves 'out on a limb' and cut off from professional colleagues and training opportunities in the psychiatric field.

Perhaps something approaching the ideal for short-term assessment and treatment has been built up by Peter Jefferys in Harrow, where he has established the right to admit his patients to the general psychiatric wards of the vast new district general hospital at Northwick Park. There is no rigid age segregation, but patients of 50+ are normally concentrated in one ward on the grounds that their tastes and habits are more likely to be compatible. This arrangement has the great advantage of easy access to all the physical facilities of the hospital for investigation and treatment, as well as easy cross-referral between the geriatric and psychogeriatric (or other specialist) departments. Functionally-ill patients can make use of the splendid facili-

ties of the general psychiatric day hospital, while those with
established dementia are taken to a specialist day hospital in the
town which they can continue to attend after discharge. Unhappily,
recent developments in Government policy make it probable that
it will become more and more difficult to obtain psychogeriatric
beds even for acute assessment and treatment in the DGHs. Yet, as
Jolley and Arie have pointed out:

'The case for the desegregation of the younger mentally ill by the
establishment of District Hospital units has been in large part a
moral case, but for elderly psychiatric patients, with their very
high prevalence of important and often treatable physical disease,
the case is a *medical* one. *Indeed, it could be argued that the first,
rather than the last group of psychiatric patients for whom provision should be made in the District General Hospitals is the
elderly.*'[8](Our italics)

Wherever the service may be provided, it is necessary to consider
whether the functionally ill should be separated from dementia
sufferers. The advantages of this policy are that the patients and
relatives of each group are not distressed by the behaviour of the
other; the functionally-ill are not confined by locked doors which
may be necessary to prevent demented patients from wandering;
nurses can give time and attention to less demanding, agitated,
depressed and withdrawn functionally-ill patients without the con-
tinual distraction of meeting the more urgent physical needs of
dementia sufferers; and differing regimes appropriate to the needs
of each group can be established. On the other hand, such segregation is likely to be wasteful of scarce resources in terms of both
space and staff and, even more important, those classified as
dementia sufferers are labelled as having a prognosis and probable
level of achievement *before* they have received the assessment and
rehabilitative treatment for which they were admitted. (If a full
assessment has been made on a domiciliary visit, this is of course
of less importance.) Another drawback is that the patient may
well be suffering from a combination of disorders—for example
depression or an acute confusional state superimposed on an early
dementia—and so fit comfortably into neither the 'functional' nor
the 'organic' diagnosis. In practice, most psychogeriatricians have
only one acute assessment ward available to them and have to do
their best to offer suitably segregated therapy within that setting
but this solution does have serious drawbacks and Godber argues
strongly for segregation as being in the interest of the patients, their

families and the provision of specialised occupational therapy and nursing care.

Relationships with other medical specialisms

If boundaries within psychiatry are complicated enough, those between psychogeriatrics and other medical specialisms are more complex still. As we have seen, old people who are mentally ill are also very often physically sick or disabled. Who should take primary responsibility for looking after them?

In 1971, the Department of Health tried to clarify this issue in a circular which put responsibility for 'elderly patients with dementia, whether mild or severe and also suffering from other significant physical disease or illness' with the geriatric departments while physically fit patients with dementia remained the responsibility of the psychiatrists. For patients whose diagnosis was mixed or uncertain, the Department advocated the setting up of integrated psychogeriatric assessment units (PGAUs).[9] However, as Godber has reported in detail, these units often ran into serious problems with silting-up because they were not adequately backed by long-stay facilities and because operational policies were often not clear and firm enough.[10] Nevertheless, if the concept of joint care is carried far enough, it can work successfully as the Department of Health Care of the Elderly in the University of Nottingham proves. This was set up *ab initio* as a joint enterprise with both medical and psychiatric wards. The professor, Tom Arie, is a psychiatrist, but he could as well be a physician or orthopaedic surgeon or could come from any other field where there is scope for a special interest in the elderly. Although the department is a unity, its services are differentiated; the staff do not believe that physicians and psychiatrists are interchangeable. The emphasis is rather on the need to collaborate closely and be readily available to each others' patients. In consequence, care can be offered according to need rather than 'label' and users of the service can come in by a single door instead of being turned away from one door and asked to try another. The unit has also proved to be a valuable teaching resource at both undergraduate and post-graduate level. Such unity of services may well be, as Arie believes, the direction in which we should move, but in the meantime a great deal can be achieved by good co-operation and collaboration between geriatrics and psychiatry.

As Jefferys has urged, 'The two specialities have to learn to respect and trust each other... Admission policies for the two services should not leave patients and their families or general practitioners in the middle between stools. In an ideal set-up the assessment by a specialist from one service about the placement of an old person requiring an acute assessment admission would be accepted as sufficient by the other service. Even where personality difficulties, geographical obstacles and inadequate resources hamper collaboration, definitions of responsibility must be compatible.'[11] This need to define responsibilities has been futher spelt out in guidelines on collaboration which have been agreed between the British Geriatrics Society and the Royal College of Psychiatrists, and which are printed as Appendix 2. The development of effective techniques of collaboration between geriatrics and psychiatry is not enough, however. As has already been pointed out, a high proportion of the patients being treated for physical illness in acute admission wards are elderly and many of these will be confused and disoriented by their admission to a totally unfamiliar environment, or suffering from depression and loss of confidence, or in an acute confusional state as a result of their illness. If they already have early dementia these symptoms will be exacerbated. It is therefore vital that physicians and surgeons on the acute wards should have a good basic understanding of mental disability in the elderly, and be ready to ask for advice from their psychiatric colleagues. It is encouraging that this has now been formally recognised by the Royal College of Physicians.[12]

Resources and training
It will be apparent that the kind of work described in this chapter cannot be done without adequate staff and facilities, but all too often, indeed almost invariably, these are not provided. D M D White, who is an experienced psychogeriatrician, say he believes this happens 'because of the complete failure of most authorities to consult in the planning stages with anyone who has a working knowledge of the psychiatry of old age. 'Psychogeriatrics' is the non-speciality of our time, and time and again it just does not seem to occur to administrators—whether at local, area or regional levels—to doubt their own abilities to "knock up" a post that "will do".'[13]

White suggests that sometimes this is done deliberately, because 'psychogeriatrics' has been made the excuse 'to create an extra post onto which is laden all the rubbish and chores of a district's psychiatric services.' More often, he believes, it happens because there is no clear model in the minds of those planning it. 'They honestly believe that psychogeriatrics is a dead-end job for which no psychiatrist in his right mind applies, and the necessity of seeking advice just does not occur to anyone.' White ends his article by setting out what he considers to be the basic requirements to make a post attractive:

'It should have the majority of its time devoted to the elderly, and any other work allocated sessions should not be likely to grow to such an extent that it impinged on the services for the elderly. There should be a reasonable share of the available beds, and some of these should be close to—or within—a department of geriatric medicine, and preferably in a general hospital. Day care facilities should exist—and not just buildings, but staff and transport for patients. A revenue sum should be available for the development of a community nursing service for the elderly. There should be a base available, with an office for the person appointed and a revenue sum for the successful candidate to appoint a secretary of his own choosing who should also have an office next door to his; a telephone is a necessity, though often forgotten. It should be clear from the material sent to potential candidates that an established psychogeriatrician had been involved with the planning—brought in from outside the region if none existed inside. It should also be seen that a local geriatric physician was involved and was on the Advisory Appointments Committee.'

The Section for the Psychiatry of Old Age at the Royal College of Psychiatrists has drawn up guidelines relating to reasonable minimum provision and these have been approved by the College's Court of Electors. They are printed as Appendix 3. However, there are very few services which operate at this level of provision and there are certainly many which get by with far less, but at the cost of immense strain, both on the psychogeriatrician concerned and on the available support services. It is not easy to hold the balance between accepting a post with inadequate back-up in the hope of developing it *in situ* and turning it down because it has not been taken sufficiently seriously by the Health Authority concerned. One way of deciding the issue is to find out whether the psychogeriatrician is being offered a fair share of the psychiatric cake. It is one thing to go short when everyone else is having to do likewise and quite another to be treated as Cinderella. Another important factor is how heavy a load the psychogeriatrician is expected to carry. Does he provide a 'dementia service' with functionally-ill elderly patients being treated by his generalist colleagues? Or is he expected to look after all elderly patients, or all new referrals over pensionable age? It is vitally important to ensure that psychogeriatricians are not isolated, over-worked and ground down until they take refuge in some less demanding speciality. Indeed, there is a great deal to be said for having two consultants working in partnership and providing each other with the moral and physical support which they need. Local pressure groups and CHCs can play a valuable part in ensuring that the relevant questions get asked and answered when a new specialist service is being established.

Even if advertised posts are properly planned, there are at present simply not enough trained psychiatrists to fill them. A survey of consultants in general psychiatry appointed between 1975 and 1978 found that 19% said they had received no training at all in psychogeriatrics, 24% felt they had not had enough, and 15% barely enough. Less than half (42%) felt that they had had sufficient.[14] There is now a requirement that psychiatrists in the registrar grade should do 6 months in this field during their 3 years' training, but in practice they can opt out if they want to. Training for consultants specialising in this field is still less satisfactory because until recently there have been no specialised senior registrar posts in psychogeriatrics and hence not even enough properly qualified candidates to succeed retiring consultants, let alone fill new posts. (Seven have now been established but these are not permanent increases and will end in about 4 years.) This explains what seems at first sight to be an extraordinarily low minimum requirement suggested by White in the article quoted above, that a candidate for a specialist consultant post 'should be able to demonstrate, apart from general psychiatric competence, that he really is interested in old people, has worked for at least a short time in an established department for the psychiatry of old age, and knows of the existence of—and preferably has visited—a few other such departments in the country'. Although the Royal College of Psychiatrists would like to insist that candidates for consultant posts should have spent at least one year at Senior Registrar level in old age psychiatry, in practice there are very few candidates who can meet this requirement and most appointment committees would be pleased to find an applicant who had a genuine commitment to the field together with general experience and at least some specialised experience in an established department.

Conclusion
This chapter about specialist psychogeriatric services has been written without making any attempt to define exactly what they are. The reason is that they can only be defined in terms of the adequacy of the service which they offer. This is not dependent on the staff

concerned having no other responsibilities. A psychogeriatrician may spend some of his time with younger patients and the same is true of social workers, community nurses and psychologists, although there is a strong view from the Royal College's Section for the Psychiatry of Old Age that the consultant with major responsibility in a district should have at least half his sessional commitment specifically designated for the elderly. Similarly, it does not depend on treatment being offered in a specialist unit. Indeed, there may be a policy decision to look after elderly patients on an acute admission ward with a complete mix of ages, as Ian Thomson does at Whitecroft Hospital on the Isle of Wight. The main point about specialisation is, as Arie has put it, 'that the *man in charge* is willing to do domiciliary visits, to take on dirty, tatty patients and see what can be done, to be positively possessive about patients who everyone else rejects'. It also means that he and his team take responsibility for spending the time, energy and skill needed to build up relationships with community services, even though generalist colleagues may also treat elderly people. It follows that one does not create a specialist psychogeriatric service simply by pinning a label on a doctor, or by lumping together the elderly patients in some huge psychiatric hospital under one consultant. There needs to be a clear decision to provide a decent service and a clear concept of how that service is to be provided. This does not demand vast outpouring of resources. The 'centres of excellence' up and down the country demonstrate that with skill and determination a little can be made to go a very long way. But that little is essential. There is a point at which both physical and human resources cannot stretch further and a service becomes 'defeated'. The beds silt up; meaningless 'waiting lists' lengthen; and staff at all levels give up trying to do a good job and settle for getting through the day. Despair creates despair. Conversely, consciousness of having a service to offer, backed by concern and enthusiasm, engenders the mobilisation of resources which multiplies many times over the value of the service provided. Ways in which this can happen are described in more detail in the next chapters of this report.

REFERENCES
1. J Wattis, L Wattis and T Arie, Psychogeriatrics: a national survey of a new branch of psychiatry. *British Medical Journal,* 282, 6275, 9 May 1980, 1529–1533.
2. R A Robinson, A comprehensive psychiatric service for the elderly, *in* J Kinnaird, J Brotherston and J Williamson (eds), *The provision of care for the elderly.* Churchill Livingstone, Edinburgh, 1981.

3. R T Woods and U P Holden, Reality orientation *in* B Isaacs (ed), *Recent advances in geriatric medicine,* Vol 2, Churchill Livingstone, Edinburgh, 1981.

4. Help the Aged, *Recall: a handbook.* Help the Aged Education Dept, London, 1981.

5. L M Jacobs, *A study of eight psychogeriatric units in Britain with particular reference to the social work support to these units.* Dept of Sociology and Social Administration, University of Southampton, 1981, (unpublished).

6. P M Jefferys, *The integration of psychiatry with services for the elderly.* Paper delivered to Royal Society of Medicine, February 6 1978 (unpublished).

7. Sharing the caring, *New Age,* Winter 1979/80, 37.

8. D J Jolley and Tom Arie, Organisation of psychogeriatric services. *British Journal of Psychiatry,* 132, 1978, 1–11.

9. Department of Health and Social Security. *Services for mental illness related to old age.* Circular HM (72) 71. DHSS, London, 1971.

10. C Godber, Conflict and collaboration between geriatric medicine and psychiatry, *in* Bernard Isaacs (ed), *Recent advances in geriatric medicine,* No. 1. Churchill Livingstone, Edinburgh, 1978.

11. See ref. 6.

12. *Organic mental impairment in the elderly: implications for research, education and the provision of services.* A report of the Royal College of Physicians by the College Committee on Geriatrics, reprinted from the *Journal of the Royal College of Physicians of London,* 15, 3, July 1981.

13. D M D White, What's wrong with psychogeriatrics? *Bulletin of the Royal College of Psychiatrists,* May 1979.

14. Peter Brook, The choice of career of consultant psychiatrists. *British Journal of Psychiatry,* 138, April 1981, 326–328.

5 Community psychiatric nurses

One important recent development in the field of psychiatry has been the emergence of the community psychiatric nurse (CPN) as a major provider of community treatment and support of mentally ill and mentally handicapped people. A survey published in 1981 found that only six health districts of the 242 who responded to a questionnaire (a 90% response rate) were without any community psychiatric nursing service, although it must be noted that levels of staffing varied widely and a quarter of all services supplied a service to districts outside their own. One hundred and fifty-four services provided a generic service only, and a further 42 (18%) also offered some form of specialist psychogeriatric care. Nearly 1800 nurses were employed either full-time or part-time in this field.[1] What is the role of this very considerable new resource, and what is its importance in relation to the psychiatric care of the elderly?

The answers, as in so many other aspects of service provision, are extremely varied. At one extreme, the CPN acts in effect as the extended arm of the psychiatrist, working closely under his supervision and carrying hospital care into the community. At the other extreme he or she is community based, taking referrals directly from the social services department and primary care teams as well as from psychiatrists and providing not only clinical nursing treatment, but also a consultative service to GPs and others concerning patients who may never be referred to a hospital. Between these two extremes every conceivable permutation and combination is possible.

Patterns of service provision
Some examples of various kinds of service will illustrate this variety. Peter Jefferys at Northwick Park Hospital, Harrow, sees trained CPNs as a scarce resource which must be used efficiently and effectively to help people who really need such skills—'not taking cups of tea with Mrs Bloggs'. Jefferys will therefore only allocate cases to his one hospital-attached CPN if there is a clear task in view, or if some emergency has arisen, such as an acute confusional episode, where immediate help and advice is required. Cases allocated to the CPN are regularly reviewed and are closed when the treatment goals have been attained. Jefferys believes it is vital to leave primary responsibility for psychogeriatric patients to the primary care team—the GPs, social workers, district nurses and health visitors—and feels that they should not be allowed to 'opt out' by referring to the CPN. In contrast, D M D White in Herefordshire operates a 'dementia service' in which he uses 10 full-time equivalent CPNs (some SRN or SEN) who do, in effect, take the primary responsi-

bility of supporting dementia sufferers off the primary care team, although they also see it as their role to mobilise and co-ordinate necessary local support. They give physical care where necessary, make domiciliary assessments (usually followed by a one-day assessment on the ward) and provide a year-round 24-hour emergency service. Somewhere between these two extremes lies the use made of specialist CPNs in Buckinghamshire. This service, which was started by White and has been further developed by H R Simons, employs 11 nurses and a nursing officer who are based in the Department of Mental Health of the Elderly, but who work closely with groups of GP practices. These GPs are encouraged to see them as part of the primary care team—'not as an extension of hospital care into the community, but rather as a community service backed up by hospital facilities'. The nurses have a consultative role and spend time talking through problems with relatives, volunteers, residential care staff, health care assistants, home helps, etc. Thus their prime role is to perform an educative function in the community, and mobilise community resources in support of their patients. In particular, they set up local voluntary day centres (described on pp 79–82) which release day hospital places for more seriously disturbed patients. They operate a standard working day at present, but if funds allowed Simons would like to see the service operating around the clock, not only to provide an emergency service, but also for such tasks as helping to get a patient ready to attend a day centre. In the services described above, the CPNs are psychogeriatric specialists, but in many other instances, they cope with the elderly as part of a mixed caseload. This can have advantages in recruitment and may make for more economic use, especially in rural areas where patients are very scattered. On the other hand, there is much to be said for the very detailed knowledge and experience which a psychogeriatric specialist can build up.

Another very different pattern of service operates with a team of community CPNs based in health centres, or similar premises and offering a service in the first instance to the primary care teams and the social service department. They may go into the psychiatric hospital for case conferences, but they do not see themselves as in any way part of the psychiatrist's team or acting under his control. The team of six CPNs, based on four health clinics in North Camden, provide an excellent example of this approach. They regard themselves as 'key workers' who are able and willing to mobilise resources in a practical way, as well as being 'detectives' who can ferret out the real nature of a problem, and 'counsellors' who are able to help people work through their difficulties. Although the service is generic, about 30% of referrals (265 in 1980) are over 65 and the bulk of referrals come from the GPs, the hospital psychiatrists preferring to use hospital-based CPNs for follow-up of their patients.

The typical shape of the two patterns of service can be expressed in diagram form:[2]

Hospital-based service

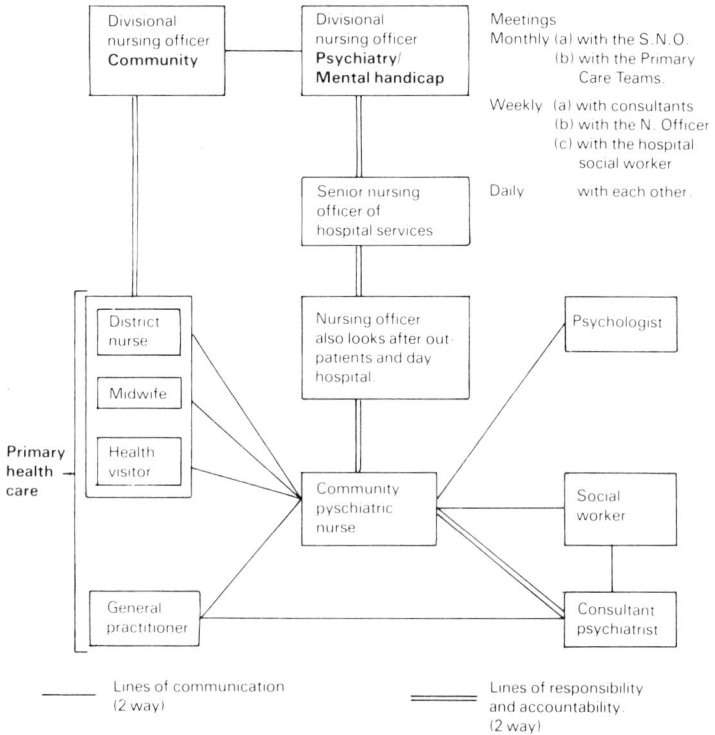

Reprinted from P J Carr et al., *Community psychiatric nursing: caring for the mentally ill and mentally handicapped in the community,* Churchill Livingstone, Edinburgh, 1980, by permission of the publishers.

There are advantages and disadvantages in both types of service. Hospital-based workers may feel that they do not have enough scope for independent action and find it more difficult to offer back-up at primary care team level. They may also feel that the senior nursing

Community-based service

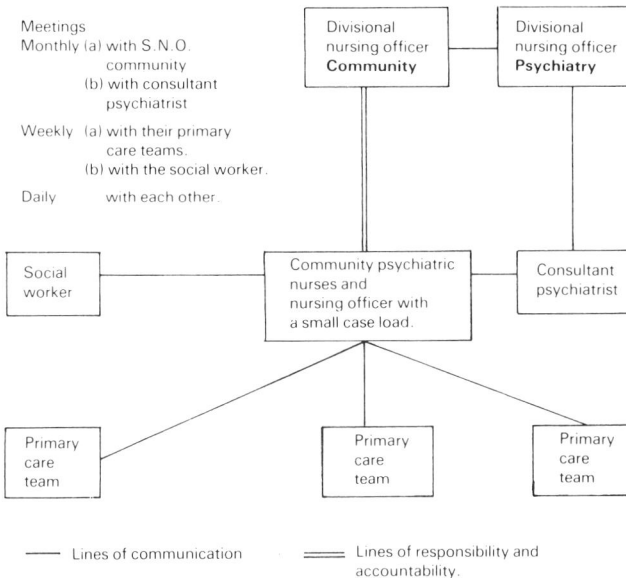

Meetings				Divisional	Divisional

Meetings
Monthly (a) with S.N.O.
        community
     (b) with consultant
        psychiatrist

Weekly (a) with their primary
        care teams.
     (b) with the social worker.

Daily   with each other.

```
Divisional            Divisional
nursing officer       nursing officer
Community             Psychiatry
```

```
Social          Community psychiatric       Consultant
worker          nurses and                  psychiatrist
                nursing officer with
                a small case load.
```

```
Primary         Primary         Primary
care            care            care
team            team            team
```

——— Lines of communication   ═══ Lines of responsibility and
                                        accountability.

officer in the hospital has little understanding of community nursing problems. On the other hand, community-based nurses may feel that they have insufficient psychiatric back-up and may find themselves carrying heavy responsibilities with little support.

Moyra Siddell, who is undertaking research on the work of specialist CPNs, lists the advantages and disadvantages of being hospital-based in these terms:[5]

Advantages
 —they know at first-hand of the patient's progress when in hospital for short-term care and can relate this knowledge to the relatives;
 —they are aware of the current bed state of the hospital and so can make realistic suggestions to supporters regarding short term care and day care;
 —they are a valuable asset to the hospital in liaising with relatives.

Disadvantages
 —they are not geographically accessible to clients;
 —they are identified with the psychiatric hospital and, therefore, the stigma which may be associated with it attaches to them;

—in times of staff shortage at the hospital, they can be called on to help, thereby neglecting their community work;

—they spend a lot of time in the hospital in meetings and adminis-tration. This is usually about two days in the hospital and three days in the community.

One solution is to provide both hospital-based and community based CPNs and to integrate their work closely with the ordinary community services. This is how Arie and Isaacs describe the service in the Goodmayes catchment area:

'In Goodmayes three nursing networks concerned predominantly with patients outside the hospital have been established. On the one hand a "community nursing unit" is based within the hospital and serves the whole hospital including the psychogeriatric unit, which is its main single client. This team of trained nurses is avail-able around-the-clock both to intervene in crises in patients' homes, and to give continuing support and make available nursing procedures. Each month the team takes some 20 new referrals from the psychogeriatric unit and makes well over 100 visits to elderly patients. Initial assessment is always by a psychiatrist, but thereafter the community nursing unit may, together with the general practitioner, take over the care of the patient at home. Great store is set on the regularity of reporting back by the nurses on all contacts with patients, and the often brief but relevant notes which complement personal discussion emphasise the importance of good communication and record-keeping on which such team-work depends.

Complementing the work of the hospital-based community nurs-ing unit are two groups of nurses based outside the hospital. On the one hand are "community psychiatric nurses" working from a district health centre, and taking referrals not only from the hos-pital but direct from family doctors and relating to whichever physician initiates the referral. On the other hand there is a liaison system with health visitors and district nurses... The extra-murally based nurses work closely with the unit, attending its meetings (in the case of the health visitors and district nurses in the person of a senior nurse who acts as liaison officer), bringing problems for discussion, taking referrals, reporting back and identifying closely with the whole enterprise.'[4]

Working conditions
Whatever the setting in which they are employed, adequate working

facilities are essential if a CPN is expected to do an effective and professional job. The DHSS report, *Organisation and management problems of mental illness hospitals*[5] (the Nodder report) lists these as being:

(a) legally accepted and professionally good practice in prescribing, administration, control, storage and transportation of drugs;
(b) access to appropriate patient records;
(c) facilities for the safe-keeping of records and reports and the preservation of confidentiality;
(d) adequate office accommodation;
(e) telephone facilities for on-call duties;
(f) adequate transport either in the form of Health Authority cars or of allowances for the use of private transport;
(g) insurance cover agreed by the Authority.

It will be seen that the role of the CPN is not an easy one. Unless she is working under the direction of a consultant who has a very clear idea of her role and keeps a firm control of her workload, she will have a heavy responsibility in defining her task and her relationships with other professionals. This is by no means a simple matter. Many GPs are reluctant to encourage CPN involvement. If they want their patients assessed, they want a consultant psychiatrist to do it; if they want services laid on, they see this as a social work role; and if they have a patient who needs intensive support, they think it should be provided in a hospital or residential home rather than in a fashion which still leaves the patient on their hands. The overlap between the roles of the social worker and CPN (whether hospital or community based) can also be problematic. The person ality and training of the individual concerned, and the resources and professional backing which she receives are therefore all-important. At its best the CPN role can provide a vital link between community and hospital, bringing specialist skills into the community which otherwise would not get to the people most in need of them, and bringing knowledge of community realities and resources into the hospital. At its worst she will be squeezed between the community and the hospital, blamed by both for the deficiencies of the other.

Training
Clearly training is needed if the full potential of this responsible and difficult job is to be realised. There is now a 9-month specialist course for psychiatric nurses working in the community which has been approved by the Joint Board of Clinical Nursing Studies

(Course 800/810) but this qualification is not legally required and carries no financial benefit. Some psychiatrists feel that it is of little value and prefer to train their CPNs themselves but professionally it is right and proper that nurses working at advanced clinical levels should receive approved and educationally-sound training. Indeed a 1977 DHSS Circular[6] described the nurse practitioner as an investigator and innovator, having knowledge of research methodology and an awareness of epidemiology as well as unusual competence in a particular speciality. It does not seem likely that these abilities can be developed adequately by informal instruction from a member of another profession.

A working party on community psychiatric nursing set up by the Royal College of Psychiatrists has this to say about training:[7]

'There is need for review of suitable training courses for those entering CP nursing. The development of shorter courses in addition to the present courses both for new entrants and for established but untrained CPNs is welcomed. In particular, there is a need for a short course for experienced CPNs or a day release type of course. If working in the community is not to become unduly separated from the rest of psychiatric nursing, all psychiatric nurses should be given an expanded period of community training. The basic nurse training should become increasingly community-orientated, so that the newly qualified psychiatric nurse can move as easily to community work as to work with in-patients, or day patients.

As with other branches of nursing, it is essential that community psychiatric nursing should develop a career structure that allows those with the interest, training and experience to remain in clinical nursing rather than have to move into administrative roles to gain promotion and increased salaries. Interchange between hospital and community work should be encouraged, but it should also be possible for relatively senior nurses to find appropriate positions for continuing their clinical work in the community.'

Between the ward and the community
The working party's suggestion that *all* Registered Mental Nurses should have some community experience and expect to be involved in work with people in their own homes is of interest. There is ample evidence that there is considerable scope for deploying hospital nurses outside their wards for crisis support, assessment and follow-up, while it is also useful for ordinary district nurses to gain

some experience of nursing demented patients in hospital. One place where this was tried out with considerable success is at Winick Hospital, near Warrington. Here a team has been built up, based on a combined geriatric/psychogeriatric assessment unit which contains nursing representatives from three separate nursing divisions—general, psychiatric and community. An appropriate member of this team undertakes all initial assessments and the team—led by a dual-trained psychiatrist/geriatrician—then decides what further action is required. This may be domiciliary assessment by the consultant, nursing care at home, or admission for in-patient assessment. The district nurses provide a good evening service, assisted by auxiliaries who give 'twilight care' and who can call out their own seniors if they need help. One of the charge nurses on the two hospital admission wards is always available to go to the home of a patient if the senior district nurse is anxious, and will, if necessary, stay all night—the charge nurse on the second ward providing cover in the hospital. Social services assist by offering an emergency bed at weekends if an acute social problem develops. Nurses coming on to the ward receive a 4-week induction training covering—'the care of the elderly mentally infirm and implementation, evaluation, needs and assessment of the individual patient, implementing preventative measures, with continuity of care in the ward, and community, with all factors and disciplines involved.' During this course, they spend two weeks with the geriatric care team, one week with the evening district nursing service, and one week accompanying the night staff when they are called out to help. Similarly, new district nurses spend a week working in the hospital, so that they not only learn the management of confused patients, but also get to know the hospital staff personally.

The service is used to support, not only the elderly mentally ill, but also people in terminal illness or elderly people who have recently been discharged from hospital. Indeed, it bears a strong resemblance to the care at home offered by hospice nurses. Its practitioners say they see their work as 'really doing the nursing process'—'they assess, treat and appraise the result of treatment'. They also see the service as offering a counterweight to the tendency of hospital care to emphasise acute treatment as opposed to on-going 'tending'. They say that the system has made it possible to free sufficient beds to provide immediate admission when this is required, and has also encouraged early referral so that crisis work has greatly diminished.

Another promising initiative in community involvement, which has unfortunately failed to survive was tried out in Denbigh Ward,

Fulbourn Hospital in the mid 1970s. This derived from an attempt by the nursing staff to develop an assessment scale schedule for recording the capacities and social functioning of patients (see p. 94). A local authority social worker became interested in using the schedule in the client's home setting and close association developed between the social work division and the ward which served it.

It became the usual practice for ward nurses to assess prospective patients in their homes as a complementary part of the usual social work assessment. At the same time, the social work department was offered two beds (later increased to seven), to which they could nominate clients for assessment or relief of supporters. Savage and Wright described the system thus:[8]

'When a social worker feels that a client would benefit by psychiatric hospital admission, they make a written assessment, in liaison with the GP. A nurse from the ward visits the patient and completes an assessment schedule. Each week the social work and nursing assessments are discussed at a meeting between the ward staff and the referring social worker. Joint decisions are made. Further social work and/or nursing help in the home setting may be recommended, or the patient may be admitted. The GP is informed. The social worker organises a client's admission and keeps in touch with the patient on the ward. This has been found to be a vital part of the service. Frequently the social worker can keep contact with the patient while working with the family by arranging for supportive services and preparing them for the client's return to the home setting.'

During a 12-month period, in which this home assessment by nurses was practised, 25 out of 62 referrals were not admitted, and of the remaining 37, 27 were discharged and four died, leaving only six to become long-stay patients. The waiting list for admission, which had been up to 3 months, disappeared and more than half the clients were admitted within a week of assessment. Apart from this major improvement in service availability, the authors of this report stated that other benefits accrued:

'The visiting and assessing of patients in their homes by ward staff, on occasions jointly with the social worker, allowed the home problems to be recognised. Equally, social workers, now knowing more about the care given to patients in the ward, were able to give a first-hand account to clients and their families in preparing them for an admission. Similarly, ward nursing staff were able to advise on the desirability of having a social work assessment as well (for example, when assessing cases referred by GPs). Thus, a degree of role sharing has been achieved by developing closer professional working relationships between nurses and social workers, while each retains his distinct, though complementary, professional skills.'

Sadly, others were less satisfied. Some of the GPs resented having their referrals vetted by nurses (especially if they were still students), and there were problems over covering the wards adequately when staff were doing assessment visits. These practical problems could have been overcome, but when a full-time psychogeriatrician replaced the part-time consultant who had previously been responsible, and who had been happy to allow nursing staff a great deal of initiative, this particular form of 'shared care' came to an end.

Conclusion

Varied as the possible ways in which a psychiatric nurse can be used outside the hospital are, one factor remains constant, and that is that their effectiveness depends on the quality of the relationships established with the hospital-based psychiatric services on the one hand, and the community-based services on the other. CPNs working with the elderly need the professional and personal ability to carry weight with their colleagues and to exercise a very considerable degree of personal judgement and initiative; they need opportunities for regular consultation with the responsible psychiatrist and appropriate Clinical Nursing Officer; they need support from the members of the nursing hierarchy who understand what work in the community involves. Above all, they need a good service to back them up. A CPN who has nothing to offer except sympathy and advice is in an impossible position and will find herself the whipping-girl for desperate families and exasperated GPs who are unable to get the help they need. At the very least, the CPN should be able to call on *quick* and competent psychiatric assessment, the provision of specialist day care for at least some days in the week and regular relief admission; the many other possible services, both voluntary and statutory, which are outlined in this report will make her work in creating appropriate and carefully thought out care packages much easier and more effective. By herself, she may be not only very limited in what she can achieve but also positively dangerous since other agencies may feel that they have solved the problem by referring cases and so accept no further responsibility.

74

REFERENCES
1. Community Psychiatric Nurses' Association, *National survey of community psychiatric nursing services.* The Association, Wigan, 1980.
2. P J Carr et al, *Community psychiatric nursing: caring for the mentally ill and mentally handicapped in the community.* Churchill Livingstone, Edinburgh, 1980.
3. Personal communication.
4. T Arie and A D Isaacs, The development of psychiatric services for the elderly in Britain *in* A D Isaacs and F Post (eds), *Studies in geriatric psychiatry.* John Wiley, Chichester, 1978.
5. DHSS, *Organisational and management problems of mental illness hospitals.* Report of a Working Group, 1980.
6. DHSS, *The extending role of the clinical nurse: legal implications and training requirements.* Circular HC/77/22. DHSS, London, 1977.
7. *Community psychiatric nursing: a discussion document by a working party of the social and community psychiatric section.* Royal College of Psychiatrists, London (undated).
8. B J Savage and A L Wright, Shared care of the elderly. *Health and Social Service Journal,* May 8, 1976, 840–841.

6 Day hospitals and day centres

Kipling's six serving men, whose names were What? and Why? and When?, How? and Where? and Who? would have had plenty to do if he had set them to work on day care and treatment for the elderly mentally ill. This service may be offered by a hospital, a local authority or a voluntary body or some combination of these. It may be an integrated part of a planned psychogeriatric service or be a facility which has 'just growed' in response to pressure on in-patient facilities or the chance availability of a building or resources. It may offer intensive short-term diagnosis and treatment facilities or long-term support; it may serve only the organically or functionally ill or cope with all comers. Apart from specialist day hospitals and day centres, facilities may also be offered in ordinary psychiatric day hospitals, in geriatric day hospitals, non-specialist day centres and workshops and in residential homes. All these settings operate their own policies regarding the nature and level of disability which they are prepared to cope with. Carter, in her extensive study of day care, found that 'the greater the need, the harder it is for an old person to get a place'. Two-thirds of the day hospitals and community-based centres which she surveyed disqualified people who were 'aggressive' or 'disruptive' and although voluntary centres and centres based in residential homes were more tolerant of this kind of behaviour, voluntary centres were less tolerant of incontinence.[1] The experience of being too disabled to qualify for help is horribly common in old age and one cannot help feeling that many facilities for the 'alert' elderly could, in fact, cope with a proportion of people with organic or functional illness if they were prepared to make the effort and if they were prepared to deal with the reality rather than the image of dementia, and look at the actual individual personality rather than the stereotype. This chapter, however, is primarily concerned with the role played by specialist day care of one kind or another and tries to sketch its potential, its limitations and its problems.

The role of the day hospital
As we have seen, thorough assessment is a crucial aspect of a psychogeriatric service and many psychiatrists believe that this can most suitably be carried out in a day hospital setting. This enables staff of various disciplines to carry out careful and unrushed observation of the patient while she is occupied in different activities. The physical examinations needed can be made with minimum stress and the patient is not confused and distressed by being admitted to a threatening and unfamiliar ward environment. However, the problem, which is so well known in ordinary geriatric day hospitals, then

arises. When the illness has been diagnosed and any active treatment completed—what next? The patient is likely by that time to have formed an attachment to the day hospital and its staff; she and her supporters enjoy the break; there may be no other facility available which will cope with her degree of disability. Should she be resolutely discharged or should she be allowed to stay on and so limit the time and facilities available to assess and treat new patients? The Brighton Clinic in Newcastle does try to pass patients on to day centres run by voluntary agencies or social services, once active psychiatric treatment and rehabilitation have been satisfactorily concluded, but even so they keep patients on average for 3 to 6 months before they begin the process of detachment and have kept patients with unstable depressive states as infrequent day hospital attenders for two or more years. Similarly the Royal Victoria Hospital in Edinburgh tries to detach gently by cutting down attendance or by encouraging a group of patients to transfer to a local authority day centre together and to attend both places for a limited time. However, as Arie points out, local authority provision is often so patchy, waiting lists so long and transport so difficult, that often no alternative is available and the day hospital therefore becomes a long-term—indeed, one might say almost a permanent—supportive facility for patients with chronic psychiatric disabilities. Discharge is much more likely to occur because some form of residential care has become imperative than because the support which the day hospital offers is no longer needed. Arie suggests that the three groups who are most suitable for psychogeriatric day care are those with organic illness who are supported at home by relatives and friends; isolated people with predominantly functional disorders 'such as chronic grumbling paranoid states or niggling depression' who are dependent on the hospital; and short-term patients who need temporary support after discharge from an in-patient unit or out-patient investigation or treatment.[2] However, as with acute in-patient wards there are problems with mixing patients with functional illness with people suffering from dementia. Indeed Jefferys takes the view that the most successful units are either totally segregated or operate an internal segregation of space and activities.

Bringing the day hospital into the community
Isolated psychiatric hospitals or even huge general hospitals are not the best place to provide day hospital care, especially for long-term patients. It may be a more effective use of resources to send NHS staff out to work in a unit which is firmly based in the community and to which relatives and community-based supporters can have

frequent and informal access. One example of this approach is provided by the Herga Day Centre in Harrow.[3] Patients with dementia
who have been admitted to hospital for assessment may be taken
daily to the unit and continue to attend after discharge, but direct
referrals are also accepted from GPs and social workers. The staff
operate with maximum flexibility. For example, they are prepared
to collect a pension or buy food for an elderly couple, with the agreement of the area social worker. Nurses regularly make domiciliary
assessment visits and see it as their job to establish close and sensi-
tive liaison with neighbours, relatives, voluntary agencies and the
primary care teams as well as with social services. One particularly
interesting initiative is the relationship established between the
Centre and the long-stay hospital wards which are based in the psychiatric hospital 14 miles away at Shenley. Staff from the hospital
visit the Centre to observe its methods and meet the patients while
the hospital is visited by Centre clients and their relatives. Much of
the fear of eventual transition to hospital care is thus alleviated.

Shrubbery Road Day Hospital, High Wycombe, is another example
of the hospital coming into the community. Here premises are
shared with a maternity unit, and a small number of relief beds
makes the provision of extended day care possible. But the hospital
also provides a working base for the CPNs who are the backbone
of this service (see pp. 64–68), and an opportunity for training
volunteers who may then move on to establish small local centres
elsewhere (see pp. 79–82). This use of volunteers in a statutory
service is itself unusual. The MIND report found that less than half
of their sample of day hospitals made use of volunteers and then on
a very small scale or only to provide transport.[4]

Volunteers can be constructively employed, however, if their use is
properly thought out. The South Western day hospital, for example,
uses a voluntary help organiser who accepts referrals for work with
particular patients, briefs volunteers and monitors progress, and
there are also two volunteers attached to the day unit and cadets and
students on training placements. The emphasis is on reliability,
thorough briefing, and the offering of the kind of help which com-
prises a service in its own right. Volunteers are not used to supplement staff or cover staff shortages. They are there to help improve
the quality of life of patients and meet social and practical needs
where no other service exists to meet those needs.[5] As is so often the
case, it is the availability of a trained professional organiser which
makes it possible to generate all this additional help in a statutory
setting and deploy it properly.

Local authority day centres

It should not be assumed that the health authorities are the only, or indeed necessarily the best source of specialist day care. Social service departments are at last beginning to take constructive interest in this field and are setting up centres which may be used for rehabilitation and assessment as well as long-term support. Close co-operation with the psychiatric services is of course essential, but the centres are usually run by people with OT and care assistant skills rather than by nurses. The atmosphere in such centres is usually relaxed and lively. One of the pleasantest experiences in preparing this report was an afternoon spent sitting in a sunny garden on a glorious June day watching clients and staff of the Highbury day centre in Birmingham swiping golf balls and knocking down skittles in an atmosphere of real enjoyment. (Although this centre shares premises with a large residential home, not one resident was to be seen in the garden.) The person in charge on the day the visit was made (actually the deputy) was a young man who had originally trained as a teacher and had then worked with mentally handicapped children. It was evident that the skills he had acquired were extremely relevant in providing a positive experience for his severely demented clientele. Care of this quality is an active and enjoyable experience, not passive 'warehousing' while the relatives have a break. We need far more small localised centres of this kind.

Local authorities may also provide day care for confused people in their residential homes. This can be an excellent facility if it is properly thought out and indeed this report argues that residential homes should be extensively used as a community resource. Too often, however, the necessary staffing, training and additional facilities are not provided and there can be resentment, conflict and sheer neglect. Carter describes how:

'Fifteen old people are transported each weekday to an old people's home in Cartown, a metropolitan district in the midlands. They sit in two gloomy sitting rooms devoid of any furnishing other than a low table and chairs backing against the walls. The only decoration in the public rooms of this home is a bowl of artificial flowers under the plaque beside the front door. No particular activities were provided for the day attenders and, as the (untrained) warden described his aim as being to 'have residents who will reflect my success in their happiness', the day users, slumped around the darkened room, slumbered on.'[6]

Contact and co-operation between day hospitals and day centres
Although there are notable exceptions, there is in general far too
little contact and co-operation between the local authority day
centres and the psychiatric services. The MIND study found that at
least half the sample of day hospitals did not know what day care
provision was being made by the local authority or by voluntary
organisations. The report goes on:

'On the whole, day hospital staff did not feel that their patients
were capable of attending social day care, as they were too infirm
and in need of a high degree of care and attention. One consultant
stated, "We do not have a great deal of liaison with them as our
patients are too handicapped to attend". Only a few tried to use
social day care facilities "as much as possible", although there was
also a feeling that most local authority provision was "over-
subscribed". In a situation where some patients will need
long-term day care, and where very little treatment can be given
medically, the whole area of day hospital provision in relation to
social day care will need to be looked at.'[7]

That is a point which cannot be too strongly emphasised.

Voluntary day centres
Specialist day centres run by volunteers with professional support
and advice are now beginning to multiply and they offer a very important resource. Their clients vary from severe dementia sufferers
at one end of the scale to social isolates who want a workshop rather
than a club at the other. Here it is only possible to give some
examples from the range of initiatives.

Age Concern Berkshire runs the Halewood Centre in Bracknell for
12 very difficult confused elderly people who, because of their
disruptive and unpredictable behaviour, have been refused local
authority care. The aim is 'to provide kindly containment, to make
the clients comfortable and provide relief for their families'. The
centre operates in a flat provided by the housing department and
is open for 5 days a week. It is hoped that evening and weekend
opening will become possible and plans are being made to use one
of the bedrooms as a short-stay emergency facility, the other bed-
room being occupied by a volunteer. There is a 1 : 1 ratio between
volunteers and clients and volunteers are carefully selected and supported. The centre works closely with the statutory authorities.[8]
Voluntary work with people as severely disabled as this is uncommon, but both MIND and Age Concern are encouraging their local

organisations to consider running specialised centres for less disabled people on one or more days a week and a number have taken up the challenge. Buckinghamshire, which has 12 such centres provides an excellent example of what can be achieved. They are set up by a combination of community psychiatric nurse (CPN) initiative and social services support, and resources now come from joint funding, Social Services Department grants and equipment, fund raising and clients' contributions. A typical centre of this kind started with a CPN identifying a group of clients who needed support. She then looked for a large village with good communications and a suitable *small* hall in the area, and opened negotiations with the committee (and still more important, the cleaner) for use of it on one day a week. Detailed discussion followed with the churches, local voluntary bodies, the GPs (who are often pessimistic about the chances of such a venture) and local people with a reputation for social energy. When the way had been thoroughly paved, a public meeting was held to explain the need and ask for all sorts of help —transport, fund raising, help on outings and contributions of furniture, cutlery, cushions, rugs, games, wool, etc.—as well as volunteers to help with the clients themselves. It was emphasised that there was no need to help for the whole day: a couple of hours in the morning or afternoon, or over the lunch period was a valuable contribution. A definite starting date was then fixed and a rota for helpers worked out, making sure that there was a generous margin of helpers to clients (1 : 2 is preferred) even if this meant a slow build up in the number of attenders. This level of staffing is considered essential to create confidence and provide a relaxed atmosphere.

Helpers were asked to attend the psychogeriatric unit for a 3-hour training session designed to help them understand the need for centres of this kind and learn basic principles of first-aid, as well as how to lift clients and assist them in the lavatory, and what to do in a crisis. At first the CPN gave extensive support and allowed leadership and commitment in the volunteers to emerge naturally. She emphasises that volunteers need to be carefully matched with the wide range of jobs which need to be done and that they often prove to have particular skills (music, craft, local knowledge) which can usefully be exploited; also that it is no use pushing volunteers or making them feel guilty when they cannot meet their commitment. Some will drop out and some 'steadies' will emerge when they have found their feet. The high ratio of volunteers to clients means that everyone can get individual attention and conversation. Volunteers may bring their own knitting and work alongside clients. Skittles and chair-based exercises (led by volunteers taught by the CPN) encourage movement. After lunch (provided by meals on wheels) and a quiet period, a regular raffle is held in which about two-thirds of the attenders get prizes and which attracts much amusement. During the day an unobtrusive eye is kept on clients' health and any attention needed for hair, eyes, feet, nails, etc., passed on to the relevant supporter. Health visitors and GPs often find it convenient to drop in and see a client while she is at the centre. During the summer a number of outings are arranged using volunteers on a 1 : 1 basis to push the wheelchairs. Transport is provided by a commercial firm and the organisers find that with a helpful driver and a lot of pulling and pushing they can manage without a tail lift.

The criteria for admission is that clients must have characteristics, whether of personality disorder, functional illness or confusion which make them unacceptable in ordinary day centres. Frequent incontinence and frequent very disturbed behaviour cannot be managed. The centre thus copes with moderate degrees of disability and so releases places for those who really do need nursing care. More important, close relationships develop between volunteers and clients which result in home visiting, hospitality and the offer of practical help. Sometimes a vicious circle of isolation and paranoia can be broken by such relationships. 'I would have adopted her as a spare granny if I hadn't been about to move' said a volunteer of one such person.

This centre has been described in detail to give an idea of what can be done by volunteers but no two centres are identical in their origins, organisation or purpose and indeed their individuality is one of their greatest assets. However, they all have in common the need for careful preparation and the availability of professional support, advice and training for the volunteers. It is especially important that volunteers working with demented people should be helped to understand the side effects of severe disorientation and also to meet the emotional needs of their clients. As Janet Mendel says of the MIND day centre project in Sheffield, 'The need is to focus on decreasing agitation and providing a calm supportive atmosphere. Activity is all very well if it is wanted, but in their mid-80s, people may not *want* to do anything. Volunteers may need help to let people just sit, and to accept regression while at the same time treating the clients as adults and not as children. Physical cuddling and the gratification of one-to-one attention may be more valuable for severely disabled people than encouraging orientation and self-determination.'

For depressed and isolated elderly people, quite different kinds of voluntary provision may be helpful. In Castleford, for example, an evening group has been set up in a geriatric day hospital which is free after 4 pm. This focuses on social isolates who live alone, have limited mobility and often suffer from depression induced by recent bereavement or loneliness. There is strong emphasis on the development of personal relationships between clients and between volunteers and clients. The authors of the journal article describing this experiment comment:

'The deprivations suffered by the elderly in our society become very real when one gets to know group members. Their sense of isolation is severe and it is clear that most of them have suffered an almost total breakdown in human contact and relationships. They cannot keep in contact with their friends because of their handicap, their spouses may have recently died and this bereavement and isolation lead to depression and loss of identity coupled with a feeling of rejection and worthlessness.'[9]

Not all people want to be sociable. Some prefer to cope with the emptiness and depression arising from bereavement or retirement by continuing to work and consider bingo and games demeaning. Work centres for the retired enabling them to make a little money and get on with a positive, even if simple job, can be of great help for chronically lonely and depressed people who are 'unclubbable'. No one should have sociability forced upon them, and volunteer initiatives in running such centres is of great value.

It will be seen from these examples that the link between professionals in the field, volunteer organisers and the volunteers themselves is a key factor in voluntary service provision. Voluntary initiatives in day care do not just happen. They need careful planning and preparation, which is almost always the job of a paid organiser or a professional who sees it as part of her role. They need enthusiastic professional support and, if the project is difficult or demanding, they need a paid organiser or an exceptionally involved volunteer to keep the project going. Given this sort of support, volunteers can cope even with people with severe dementia, provided the ratio of volunteers to clients is kept at a generous level, and they certainly have a great deal to offer less severely disabled people.

Day care as support for supporters
The point has already been made that day care by itself cannot

always offer adequate support for people with severe dementia who are living by themselves. It is, however, of immense value when they are living with supporting relatives since it enables the relatives to have a regular break or to go on working and thus to go on caring. But if this is, as it ought to be, a primary objective of day care, is the standard provision of 10 am–4 pm from Monday to Friday sufficient to make any real difference? What of daughters who can cope during the week, but want to be free to attend to the needs of their husbands and children at weekends? Or those who can cope by day when the family is out of the house, but find the combination of elderly parent and boisterous children too difficult in the evenings?

In this connection the comment of a professional woman looking after an elderly mother-in-law with dementia is of interest. The old lady had been discharged from hospital at the age of 92 and was no longer able to cope at home. She was being cared for by her daughter-in-law pending admission to residential care, but the carer was torn between her exasperation at the old lady's constant demands and her own need to get back to work, on the one hand, and her guilt at putting her into a home on the other. She told a neighbour:

'I could cope ... It would be possible if there were genuine day centres for the senile. Not glorified lunch clubs where the ambulances collect at 10.30 and have them home for 3.00. I mean a place where I could run granny at 8.30 and then pick her up after work. Like your full day centre for toddlers, as opposed to nursery school; a place that would let you work. Or there might be a neighbourhood house for the old, like the children's house in a kibbutz. We could collect them each evening. Only it should accept all the elderly in need, not make these fine distinctions between the physically handicapped and the senile, ambulant and non-ambulant, that the selection committees seem to love. Ever finer combs, just when we're under pressure in the schools to teach all kids together. It'd be cheaper than a full residential home, and allay family guilt.'[10]

Both Arie[11] and Greene and Timbury[12] make the same point in more measured terms.

In one or two places, services of this kind are developing. The Shrubbery Road Day Hospital in High Wycombe combines day care with short-term relief beds and 24-hour nursing cover so that it can offer supporters completely flexible hours of care, for example, and Jeffreys, in Harrow, has on his 'shopping list' the use of the Herga Centre for weekend support. Day care in a hospital or residential home also makes it possible to keep people later or admit them earlier than is feasible in an independent facility but transport problems are often a limiting factor (see p. 85).

Day hospital care (as opposed to local authority centres) is not without its risks. Admission may give relatives and other supporters (including the GP, the social worker and the community nurse) the impression that the hospital has taken over responsibility and they need not bother any longer. Clearly, the way in which contact with relatives or other supporters is established and maintained is a vital factor in preventing this and there is evidence that far too little attention is paid to this issue. The MIND report states that of the 27 day hospitals studied, 18 had no formal procedures for establishing contact with supporters,[13] while Carter found 'that although offering day care to old people was seen by some heads and staff as a relief to relatives, this was not associated with actual contact between the unit staff and the relatives. In the main, such contact in geriatric and psychogeriatric day units was *ad hoc,* unplanned and infrequent'. Admission procedures to units for the elderly rarely included interviews with family members and a home visit by day hospital staff before admission was very uncommon.[14]

Certainly day hospitals (and day centres) could pay much more attention to their admission procedures. Most confused old people are nervous of a new experience and may refuse to attend unless time and effort is given to introduce them and their key supporters to the unit and working out a treatment alliance. For example at the Herga Centre in Harrow a new patient and her relatives are invited to make a short preliminary visit, often escorted by a CPN or social worker, and a careful introduction to the team who run the centre takes place over coffee. This is a great help in enabling the patient and her family to negotiate a realistic initial treatment contract. However, although it is very important to establish initial contact with relatives and remain available to them it is also important to remember that relatives may justifiably regard day hospitals as places which have, albeit temporarily, taken over all responsibility and they may prefer to know as little as possible about what goes on there, since they have enough to cope with for the rest of the time. It is also necessary to remember that some relatives may only be able to bear the emotional stress of providing support for a dementia sufferer by a mental withdrawal and so be threatened by a day hospital which seeks to re-establish relationships which are, in effect, already dead. Urging 24-hour reality orientation, for example, on a daughter who can only cope by treating her mother as a mindless body may make her decide that she cannot cope at all. We will know more about supporters' attitudes to day hospitals and the kind of service which they find most helpful when Chris Gilleard publishes the full results of his current research into this topic.[15]

Transport
The one subject on which everyone is agreed is that transport problems are a critical bottleneck in operating and extending day care services. Many day hospital places are not filled, and whole units remain unopened because patients cannot be brought in. Those who do come may be delivered so late and collected so early that time for any effective therapy is severely limited and the time of expensive professional staff is wasted. Thus, the MIND survey found that, although hospitals in their sample were open on average for 8 hours a day, the time patients spent there was sometimes as little as $3\frac{1}{2}$ hours.[16] And Arie says that when he was at Goodmayes Hospital the day patients coming from the more distant parts of the catchment area spent almost as long in the ambulance as at the hospital. He adds only half jokingly in an often-quoted passage:

'It has occurred to us to wonder whether we should not claim a new form of psychiatric treatment known as "transport therapy". In this, the exigencies of the transport system are made into a virtue (or what is even more than a virtue, a treatment) and the patient is jogged along the countryside for several hours. In "transport therapy", in keeping with the fashionable emphasis on keeping people out of hospital, the hospital becomes irrelevant and to travel happily becomes more important than to arrive. Meals can be taken at a friendly transport cafe, always provided there is a greater-than-average provision of functioning lavatories.'[17]

If transport is provided by the ambulance service, patients are competing for vehicles and drivers with the demands of the emergency service and the out-patient clinics so that a spate of accidents on an icy day or unusual demand from an out-patient clinic can result in day patients not being picked up at all. This unreliability can make patients and their relatives prefer complete non-attendance to uncertainty. Strikes are, of course, more damaging still. MIND quotes David Jolley of the Withington Hospital, South Manchester, as saying that a strike had placed those providing day care in a situation where they could in no way keep the promises that they had made to clients and their relatives. 'Already one is aware of tremendous disheartenment and concern amongst those families who have supported people in the community with the help of nurses and the day hospital, who feel now that the only reliable way that their relatives can be managed is by recourse to admission on a permanent basis.'[18] Transport facilities also limit the extent to which flexible hours can be offered, since early delivery or late collection is not likely to fit in with drivers' shifts and overtime rates are prohibitively expensive. None of these difficulties is insurmountable, given sufficient effort and motivation. The non-emergency ambulance service can be misused because some hospital staff do not take the trouble to check that transport provision for out-patients or patients being admitted and discharged is really necessary. Carelessness in giving instructions, failure to cancel an order, keeping transport hanging about while the patient is found or a late clinic is finished—all these and many more causes of waste have been identified.[19] On the ambulance side, failure to use modern methods of fleet control, poor management and union disputes also cause waste and inefficiency. Psychiatrists whose work is ham-strung by transport difficulties could push harder than they do to make sure that their colleagues in other fields (particularly geriatricians and orthopaedic surgeons) keep tight control on their use of the service and stagger especially demanding clinics. There is also a strong case for putting elderly day hospital patients next to accident and emergency use in the list of priorities, as an NHS working party report has recommended.[20] An out-patient can, if the worst comes to the worst, make another appointment. An elderly demented person whose carers think she is safely at a hospital can die for lack of transport.

Some units operate with their own vehicles and their own drivers, using them for other duties during the middle of the day. This is excellent, provided the catchment area is reasonably compact and the vehicle keeps going. However, a breakdown can cause very serious problems, whereas an ordinary ambulance driver can simply radio for a substitute. Some well-established day care hospitals have acquired services which were running before re-organisation and are, therefore, accepted by the unions and administrators. The Forest Day Hospital in Leicestershire, for example, has made extensive use of taxis and finds that the flexible and personal service which they offer is very satisfactory for ambulant patients. In Brighton the Bevendean Day Hospital has drivers especially seconded to the job by the ambulance service who are not fully trained and, therefore, cannot be used for emergency work. These drivers develop a close relationship with the patients and the unit's staff; they provide a channel of communication between staff and relatives; contact the day hospital if the patient is too ill to attend; and on numerous occasions have helped the patient to dress. The Herga Day Centre in Harrow had initial difficulties in persuading the service that it was not 'just a social club for ordinary old people'. But having done so, it now has regular drivers seconded for its use who are regarded as key members of the team and who collect patients with the regular help of a nurse attendant. This is probably the ideal solution if it can be negotiated.

Ambulances are, of course, not the only form of transport in common use. Volunteer services of various kinds, social services minibuses, hired minibuses and taxis all play a part. These facilities are expensive however; even volunteers driving their own cars now have to claim a heavy mileage allowance if they are not to be out of pocket. Also social services transport, like the ambulance service, has problems of competition between different users during the morning and evening peaks, and the elderly often lose out.

The best answer to transport problems is to keep day centres small and local. If a confused person has forgotten the day when her transport calls, it is easy to drop the other passengers at the centre and go back for her if she lives close by. Short distances minimise the length of 'transport therapy' and maximise the use made of hospital or centre facilities. More clients will be able to walk in, perhaps having been collected by a member of staff or a volunteer. Costs are kept down and if journeys are short, the statutory services are more likely to be co-operative about helping out. As this report shows, there is a great deal of scope for developing local day care, and we should be making a virtue of necessity rather than constantly grumbling about the stranglehold created by transport shortages.

Conclusion
Day care is not a magical solution to all the problems of treating and supporting mentally-ill old people. In particular, it may be inadequate for those with severe dementia who are living alone. For those with caring relatives, however, day care can offer a heaven sent break and for those in the early stages of dementia day care can do a great deal to slow down deterioration and alleviate its social consequences. For the depressed and isolated, the paranoid and deluded, day care can offer a lifeline back to social involvement and self confidence. For those who need assessment and treatment without the trauma of hospital admission, day hospitals are invaluable. Though not a cure-all, day care is an essential part of our service

88

for mentally-ill elderly people and we should be doing everything possible to extend its availability and its flexibility.

REFERENCES

1. Jan Carter, *Day services for adults: somewhere to go.* George Allen and Unwin, London, 1981.
2. T Arie, Day care in geriatric psychiatry. *Gerontologia Clinica,* 17, 1975, 31–39.
3. MIND, *Approaches to day care: for elderly people who are mentally ill.* MIND, London, 1979.
4. Sheila M Peace, *Caring from day to day: a report on the development of the day hospital within the service for elderly people who are mentally infirm.* MIND, London, 1979.
5. See ref. 3.
6. See ref. 1.
7. See ref. 4.
8. Further information available from Age Concern, Marsh Court, Wilton Road, Reading, Berks.
9. Malcolm M Hornby and Mike Brown, The night comes alive with the sound of laughter. *Health and Social Service Journal,* 89, 4662, October 5 1979, 1286–1287.
10. Annis Fleur, Looking after granny: the reality of community care. *New Society,* 54, 934, October 9 1980, 56–58.
11. See ref. 2.
12. J G Greene and G C Timbury, A geriatric psychiatry day hospital service: a five-year review. *Age and Ageing,* 8, 1, 1979, 49–53.
13. See ref. 4.
14. See ref. 1.
15. C J Gilleard, G Watt and W D Boyd, *Problems of caring for the elderly mentally infirm at home.* Paper presented at the XII International Congress of Gerontology, July 12–17, 1981, Hamburg, West Germany (Report of the pilot studies).
16. See ref. 4.
17. See ref. 2.
18. See ref. 4.
19. A J Norman, *Outpatient ambulance transport: conference report.* National Corporation for the Care of Old People, London, 1978 and A J Norman, *'Need' for an ambulance: conference report.* Beth Johnson Foundation and NCCOP, London, 1979. Obtainable from Centre for Policy on Ageing, London.
20. Patient Transport Services Working Party, for the NHS Sheffield, *Patient transport services: a report of a working party.* Trent Regional Health Authority, Sheffield, 1981.

7 Longer-term hospital care

One of the basic themes of this report is that we need to hold a creative tension between providing appropriate care for chronically-mentally disabled elderly people in the community on the one hand, and maintaining sufficient hospital beds on the other. Too many beds may be counter-productive in that they weaken the drive to build up community-based resources and especially good relationships with residential homes. Too few beds mean that the vital facility of regular relief admission and crisis admission cannot be provided on an adequate level and that long-term admission cannot be offered until community support, whether of relatives, neighbours, home helps or care staff has been overstretched to a level which can amount to cruelty. Also, it can be argued that too tough an attitude towards long-term admission is wasteful in resources, in that a great deal of work is needed to prop up a really precarious support system, and this will probably only be successful for a short time. This report argues in the next chapter that most elderly people who need long-term care can and should be looked after in residential homes, but there will always be some patients who for one reason or another really do need long-term hospital care, and putting sufficient resources into the residential care sector to enable it to cope with the remainder will inevitably be a long and complex process. This chapter looks at what can be done to make the lives of those who live in these wards, and the jobs of those who work there as fulfilling as possible.

No one would pretend it is an easy task and some would claim that it is impossible. We all know of wards which are ill-maintained, overcrowded and shabby with broken, out-of-date facilities; wards in which low prestige, minimal resources and staff who are inadequate in both numbers and training create a vicious circle which it seems almost impossible to break. There are no simple answers and no single answer. Big institutions have lives of their own, and breaking their bad habits is an immensely difficult and complex process which demands not only informed and skilful leadership, and nursing staff who are able and willing to shift their perceptions and re-think their roles, but also understanding and support from a wide range of ancillary staff—maintenance men, domestics, administrators, trades union officials, as well as occupational therapists, physiotherapists and psychologists. It may also require changes in the expectations of related institutions or other parts of the same institution concerning the proper role of the wards concerned, and the way in which that role should be fulfilled. Manipulating one little bit of the system by introducing a 'hit and run' expert or

90

decreeing cosmetic alternations in furnishings and routines will not, by themselves, produce lasting change. Nevertheless, though it would be foolish to under-rate the difficulties, it is defeatist to be overwhelmed by them and the literature is full of examples of what can be done.

Leadership and integration
One of the major problems of long-stay wards is that they are all too often segregated—mentally, administratively and often geographically—from acute admission and treatment facilities, and the patients in them are regarded as having reached the end of the road —'warehoused', to be kept clean and fed until they die but at the end of the queue for financial resources and skilled staff time. Indeed, Tony Whitehead at Bevendean Hospital, Brighton, believes that the very labelling of wards or patients as 'long-stay' makes it impossible to maintain therapeutic optimism and effort and so uses the two wards available to him as a totally-mixed admission, treatment, rehabilitation and long-stay facility. At any one time two-thirds of the patients are medium or long-stay but many of the so-called long-stay patients are eventually discharged when in the past they would have been transferred to the psychiatric hospital and stayed there. Even if this approach is not practicable it remains essential for the responsible consultant to give the kind of leadership and show the kind of interest which will convince staff that he knows and cares about them and their patients and the quality of care which they provide and that their place in the psychogeriatric service is understood and valued. If a psychogeriatric service is to maintain efficiency and morale, it must be run as a whole and not with the section which is primarily concerned with providing nursing care feeling like, and being treated as, a rubbish dump. For this reason, there must be serious doubts about the DHSS's official policy of hiving off patients who are deemed not to need the facilities of the DGHs into local long-stay hospitals or NHS nursing homes. If, as is suggested in Chapter 8, the staff of residential homes are trained and equipped to cope with all but the most difficult and dependent old people, the remainder should be cared for in a setting where their well-being can be properly sustained.

Creative nursing roles
Paradoxically, medical care and concern needs to be demonstrated by maximum delegation of responsibility to the nursing staff and the encouragement of a relaxed, creative, experimental approach to the way in which wards are run and the objectives of care are defined. Psychogeriatric nursing can mean teaching, observing, running

therapeutic groups, art classes and music sessions, re-ordering the environment, and reacting to relatives as well as physical caring. The following examples all taken from actual practice, show what *can* be done.

The nurse as a teacher
David Jolley describes how Frank Parker, an ex-headmaster working at Carlton Hayes Hospital, encouraged nurses to treat the learning difficulties of their patients in the same way as they would educationally subnormal children. Selected patients were split off into a group of 6–8 and given their own side-rooms and separate sitting and dining area. Staff were encouraged to verbalise all procedures and provide incentives for self-care, using a great deal of praise and other behavioural rewards. Parker's final report stated:

'At the beginning all the patients were unresponsive, apathetic, perseverating and vacant. None was an individual person viewed from the door, all were a ward group. Some needed much help. In 8 weeks mannerisms had minimised, folk looked to see who had come into the ward, they moved within the ward, incontinence did not exist. In 12 weeks all were said to be eating less, all had lost weight and were judged to be in better physical shape. In 18 weeks, occupations had been established about which some could converse. Greater recall was evident in all patients. At the end of the 6 months, no patient had died. Chair-bound patients were moving voluntarily, self-help at meals was established and an identity within the group and of the group, plus its nurses distinct from the rest of the community at social functions outside the hospital, was well established.'[1]

(We are not told what happened to this privileged group of patients after the experiment ended or what was done to spread the use of these techniques more widely in the hospital.)

The nurse as a reinforcer of reality
The approach described above appears to be very similar in practice to the techniques which come under the umbrella title of '24-hour reality orientation' (24-hour RO). This approach, as Hanley describes it, is focused on 'the attitudes, expectations and behaviour of all those who come in contact with the confused person'.[2] All contacts with a patient (or a resident) are used to remind him or her where he is, to explain what is happening, and to encourage self-initiated and directed activity, while furniture and decor are also modified to make orientation as easy as possible.

This is how the occupational therapist describes the application of 24-hour RO on a 20-bedded short-stay relief admission ward at Moorgreen Hospital, Southampton:[3]

'The patients sit beside their bed for breakfast, in dressing gown and slippers. OT helpers (who are used as well as nursing auxiliaries on this ward) are assigned to 2 or 3 patients for a week at a time and are expected to do all routine care and encourage patients. During their time with the patient, they are to talk to the patient about the process of dressing and who they are, where they are and what day it is. There are multi-coloured boards on the lockers and on the beds with the patient's name written in upper and lower-case letters with washable felt-tip pen. Other clues that we've found helpful to supply for our patients (and ourselves) include specially coloured doors and large labels in upper and lower-case letters for such patient use areas as lounge, dining-room, mens' beds and ladies' beds. . .

All toilet doors were painted yellow and there is yellow tape on the floor and the handrail to the toilet—so it's "follow the yellow lines to the yellow door—that's the toilet".

At the physiotherapy helper's request, some patients are left sitting beside their bed for her to walk, others will make their own way up the corridor or have some assistance. There is a large clock with big numbers, two calendars and an RO board—a white metal board with magnetic letters spelling out:

> This is Durley Ward
> Moorgreen Hospital
> West End
> Southampton
> Today is Friday, March 16th, 1979.

Supper menus are also written out on a small blackboard. There are two daily newspapers. . . And so it goes on throughout the day: factual, orientating information, repeated at every opportunity, asking for an appropriate response from the patient—giving praise when it happens. Things can get a bit frantic when an old lady insists on going out to get something in for the children's tea and you gently point out that she is in hospital; that a meal will be provided—"See, there will be Cornish Pasties, creamed potatoes and coffee mousse". There is no guarantee that an anxious or agitated woman will take any notice of promises of coffee mousse. However, an explanation has been made, a distraction or diversion offered and the responses to the patient have been honest and consistent.'

Honesty and consistency are of vital importance when trying to implement 24-hour RO. It is essential that goals of achievement should be set for each person and that all the staff concerned with her should know what these are. It is no use if one morning she is encouraged to select garments in an appropriate order and put them on with minimal assistance, while on another morning she has them handed to her, and the third day is dressed like a baby. The same is true of all aspects of daily living. To achieve such consistency in practice is by no means easy and involves a high level of staff training and participation, as well as sufficient staff to have the time (and patience) necessary. It also requires a relaxed unrigid regime where mealtimes and toiletting fit patients' needs and not vice-versa. It seems likely that many institutions claim to operate 24-hour RO, when in fact they are doing little more than encouraging staff to talk to patients and putting up the odd clock and calendar. Conversely, good institutions may, in fact, be operating on this basis as a matter of courtesy and common-sense without using grand-sounding names. This, as Woods points out, can make it very difficult to measure the effects of introducing 24-hour RO in any scientific way. There is no doubt, however, that rigid and uncommunicative institutional regimes do exacerbate the effects of dementia and that changes of the kind outlined above can produce a beneficial circle of greater patient happiness and independence and higher staff morale.

The nurse as an observer
Genuine changes in professional behaviour and in institutional regimes can only be introduced with much patience, care and perseverance. It is not enough, as was noted above, to introduce a hit-and-run expert for a few weeks. Good leadership is certainly essential and so is external co-operation, but the basic starting point is to try to promote staff awareness of what they are actually doing. A particularly well-written up example of such an exercise is provided by the Denbigh psychogeriatric admission ward (which had been badly silted-up) at the huge, understaffed and overpressed Fulbourn psychiatric hospital near Cambridge. Here the nurses first set themselves to answer the questions:

(i) What do we spend our time doing? And how much time do we spend doing it?

94

(ii) What difference does high and low staffing make?
(iii) What is the difference between week-ends and week-days?

To achieve this, they broke down their activities into 27 broad categories and every 15 minutes for 11 days noted the category of activity in which they had been mainly engaged. The results showed them that 'staff time' (i.e. discussion about patients, handover meetings, etc) was the most time-consuming single category, and that the timetable too often required all the patients to be doing the same thing at the same time with the result that the staff available to help them were overpressed. As a result of this new insight, steps were taken to change the routine. Breakfast time, for example became variable according to the dependency of the patient, and day staff became willing to get patients up at a reasonable hour, with the result that patients slept better and there was less wandering at night. The time of high tea was changed from 4.00 to 6.00 pm, so a more normal eating pattern could be established (this required the help of a co-operative superintendent who was able to find someone to wash up); patients could be encouraged to participate in household activity because it had become less important to get everything done perfectly and on time; and communication with individual patients became concentrated on achieving particular goals. This, in turn led to detailed assessment of patient abilities and from there to involvement in community assessment, and close co-operation with the community social workers (see pp. 71–73).[4] In this instance, the impetus for change came from an exceptional charge nurse and a social psychologist based in the hospital who saw effecting and observing change as his principal role, while important back-up was provided by the consultant.

The nurse as a group worker
The therapeutic use of the daily routine and the whole environment does not, of course, exclude the use of groups for specific purposes and many of the group activities described in Chapter 4 can be of great value, both in enhancing the lives and alertness of patients and in encouraging other changes. Veronica Coulshed (a social worker) describes how she introduced classroom reality orientation run by nurses into a ward where there was 'understaffing, poor morale, minimum contact with patients and a general sense of hopelessness'. These 'classroom' groups were supplemented by nurses' discussion groups at which various aspects of the care of the elderly were debated and information about the new experience exchanged. The RO soon widened into 24-hour activity, the establishment of a relatives' group, frequent outings to the neighbourhood and person-

alised nursing care which benefited the very frail, deaf or restless patients who were unsuited for group activity. There was a general improvement in orientation and independence and in the interest in the ward from relatives, doctors and paramedical staff.[5]

Similarly, the introduction of classroom RO sessions at Plympton Hospital, Plymouth (after very careful preparation and with a psychologist's help) brought considerable secondary benefits.

'The ward staff emphasised that the sessions were opportunities for them to relate to patients as they wished. Typical comments were: "It brings staff and patients closer together." "You have more interest in the patient as a person." "The patients are treated as individuals and not just as a number." "We knew our patients were individuals, but we didn't know how individual they were." The fact that sessions were planned as part of the ward programme reduced the nurse's conflict about whether she should be "just sitting listening". Even so, there was frustration at times when sessions had to be brought to a rapid end because of other responsibilities. Nurses had become more aware of the pressure on their time, and saw the advantages of a group where there was time really to listen to patients—"you discover the benefits of waiting to hear what the patient is thinking".

The staff were fascinated by the aspects of life that the patients revealed. Here were people who had worked, fought in wars, taken responsibility, often before the staff were born. One woman had worked in a jam factory for 2s/6d a week, and had supplemented her low wages by carrying out pots of jam in her undergarments; another was a laundress and seamstress who overcharged her wealthier clients so that she need not take money from the poorer families. The nurses shared the sadder moments; the poignancy of a person who had shopped and collected pensions for old people—and suddenly found she needed someone to do these things for her; the difficulty of coming to terms with the loss of loved ones, of familiar objects, of pets that had to be put down when the person came into hospital. Staff as well as patients talked about themselves and a relationship developed in which the nurses were recognised as individuals with families, homes and outside interests. For some nurses this was a fairly major change and one or two commented that this went against their training; "you were told never to become involved".'[6]

The value of relatives' groups does not cease when a person is admitted to long-term care. Indeed, it may be after this has happened that support is most needed. The sense of failure and guilt at having to give up responsibility can be acute and there is a danger of this being transferred to nursing or care staff so that relatives produce a stream of complaints about inadequate care and then staff retaliate. These relatives are coping with the death of a personality before the death of a body. They need help to accept the reality of the situation and also to go on feeling that they are doing what can be done in offering love and support, even if 'it's not my husband any longer'.

It is not only relatives who can gain from staff/relative interaction. Leeming and Luke describe a series of meetings between relatives and staff relating to 33 very frail and disabled geriatric in-patients, 9 of whom could not converse at all because of deafness, dementia, aphasia or dysarthia. About eight patients were discussed with invited relatives at each meeting:

> 'There were many points of medical and nursing interest, but discussion ranged widely to include patients' personalities, past behaviour, and family and social circumstances. Aspects of day-to-day condition at the time, whether everything had been done to ensure a patient's comfort when sitting out of bed and whether a daughter could accompany her mother to give moral support when she was referred to another consultant for advice. An interesting observation, in view of the patients' mental frailty, was that an unusual treat, such as an unexpected visitor or the gift of an especially fancied food, a fresh peach for example, would be remembered weeks later.'

From information given by relatives about past interests and hobbies, it was possible to develop activities such as gardening on raised flower beds and listening to classical music while on one occasion staff and patients joined forces at a tea party, the relatives helping with the transport of patients from the wards to the day hospital and bringing in food from home, while the staff played only a minor role. 'The tea party became very much a family affair when as many as four relatives of differing ages sat in a group with a patient, who resumed her role as "head of the table" with obvious relish'.[7]

Painting is an underused therapy for dementia patients. Hamilton and Simon describe how art therapy, defined as 'the undirected and spontaneous use of drawing and painting' helped 14 patients from a long-stay geriatric ward of whom 4 suffered from dementia and 5 were depressed, as well as suffering physical disabilities. The patients were divided into 2 groups of 7 and worked together for 1 to $1\frac{1}{2}$ hours each week in a small room set apart for art therapy.

Before the start of the 6 month period, each participant was allotted a numerical score of 0–36 depending on his or her performance with the Modified Royal College Mental Test.

'The group had little difficulty in starting to paint or draw, although most lacked the power to continue without regular encouragement. This was given by inviting value judgments; if an old person indicated confusion by putting down the brush, trying to "smoke" pastels, or fold the paper, he was asked if he liked the colour he had used, or the effect of the chalk, or would like a change. By drawing attention to the effects they had already created and their power to alter them, it was possible to extend the patients' interest until most of them were actively participating and expressing pleasure in the results.

Mrs B, an old lady of 92 who scored 7 in the first assessment, is an example of a natural painter. She normally spent all day in the ward with her eyes shut, tapping the tray of her wheelchair and making so much noise that she could not be tolerated in the day room. When she first came to art therapy and was given a brush loaded with paint, she began to tap until her attention was directed to the paint marks she had inadvertently made. At once she indicated strong preferences for certain colours which she arranged aesthetically, building up her picture by over-painting. When asked about her work Mrs B said: "I just couldn't tell you. It's quite—early. Where we can all go for our reasonable life... The pink is very nice and we'll have more room for the ... The clouds are too high—but the other blue is top-heavy. The white is nice and clean." These remarks suggest that she saw her painting as landscape. Although she did not remember the art therapists from week to week, she showed no difficulty in recognising her previous week's work in the pile... Other patients showed a conceptual approach to the work and developed their ideas week by week, sometimes planning several days ahead. Thus, Mrs H, who suffered from dementia, produced a drawing representing her childhood teacher and ideal; she drew details of her hair and clothes and wrote a page of reminiscences. The nursing staff did not know that she had retained these abilities.'[8]

Music can also be of great value. People with dementia often retain the ability to recognise familiar tunes, to sing and to keep time after many other faculties have disappeared. Thus, a session with familiar records, singing, dancing and perhaps playing some percussion instruments can be a very lively occasion.

In all these examples, it will be observed that other professionals have played an enabling role, including a teacher, an occupational therapist, a social psychologist, a social worker, a clinical psychologist and an art therapist. A physiotherapist could well have been included also, since maintaining maximum physical capacity in psychiatric patients is an essential aspect of their care and often a very neglected one. It is vital that nursing staff should have the professional advice and support which they need to review their own roles and to establish properly worked out programmes of care. It is equally vital that these professionals should play an *enabling* role and not take over all the exciting and enjoyable work while the nurses are left with the mopping up. If teamwork is to mean anything, it means that skills are shared. One cannot chop individuals up into pieces and farm the bits out to the relevant experts, and it is nurses as the basic care providers who need to have both the opportunity and the willingness to acquire the insights of other professions and apply them, backed by all the help and support which they need to do so. In a sense, all these professions (including medicine) are as a Senior Clinical Psychologist has pointed out, 'professions supplementary to nursing'.[9]

Staffing

No doubt many readers will protest that all this is pie-in-the-sky, and that with acute staffing problems and the difficulties of extracting the most basic amenities from the administration, custodial care is all that can be expected. No one would underestimate the problems, but some comments on them may be useful. First, nurses are no longer the helpless subjects of consultants. It is true that Parkinson's law will always ensure that all available long-stay psychogeriatric beds are filled, but if wards are overcrowded and understaffed, so that proper care cannot be given, nurses have both a right and a duty to do something about it. The enquiry into St Augustine's Hospital referred to 'the widespread, but erroneous belief throughout the hospital that no bed can be taken down unless the consultant agrees'. It went on:

> 'There must be an end to this wrong thinking. The consultant does not own the bed and has no more authority over it than the nurse. It should be an essential part of ward policy that there is an *agreement* between medical and nursing staff on the number of patients on any one ward, the function of the ward, and the rate of admission, if it is an admission ward. Where it is not possible to reach agreement at ward level, the problem should be referred to the Clinical Area Multidisciplinary Team and from

there, if necessary, to the Hospital Management Team. Failing agreement within the hospital, the problem must be taken to the District Management Team, and from there to the Area Health Authority and ultimately, if need be, to the Region. There are many hospitals with wards containing too many patients. Where no immediate reduction is possible, it should at least be possible to agree forward plans, including the rate at which beds will be taken down and the eventual totals. Monitoring of the progress is an essential part of the job of both the Hospital Management Team and the District Management Team.'[10]

Nursing 'work'

Second, there is considerable evidence that better staffing levels will not, of themselves, automatically produce improved levels of activity or of staff/patient interaction. Godlove's study, *Time for action,* compared interaction in a hospital ward, a day hospital, a day centre and a local authority home (with comparable levels of disability in each) and found that:

'For more than 20% of the time, the staff-patient ratio in hospital wards was 1 : 2 or better. This was a higher percentage than the equivalent figure for any of the other three environments and yet there was less contact with staff than in day hospitals and a higher proportion of time spent in isolated inactivity than anywhere else.'[11]

This observation is borne out by an earlier study by May Clarke which found that:

'Work in industrial society has come to mean an activity people do during the time they are paid for, and the nurses' belief that what properly constituted work involved "doing" something in the sense of expending physical energy was probably formed externally to the hospital situation. But the organisation of work in many parts of the hospital reinforced this. It was on their performance of physical tasks that nurses felt that they would be judged and sanctioned and, in the circumstances, talking or listening or waiting for a patient to do something for herself was considered less work-like than doing something for her, such as bathing and dressing. Nurses tended to believe that if they were not seen to be doing something, "someone, somewhere would complain that they were not really working." '[12]

This physically-oriented concept of 'work' is easily reinforced by an assumption that the nursing task on long-stay wards is not to prevent increasing dependency, but to give good basic care, and to keep the patients dry and fed. The ward ethos may, in fact, encourage regressed behaviour. Clarke comments in another study that incontinence was accepted as normal:

'It was dealt with in a kindly, cheerful way and the use of disposable incontinence sheets allowed the problem to be contained within reasonable limits. There were, on the other hand, no rewards for patients who could remain continent and who asked to go to the lavatory. Usually they were offered a commode on which they were very conspicuous and which caused more problems for the nursing staff than if they had been incontinent.'[13]

Thus, although there is ample evidence that good nursing care can have a dramatic effect in reducing incontinence, it is clear that staff must be very clearly and strongly motivated if they are not to take an easier way out and nurse their patients as if they were babies.

Another factor in the perceived weight of 'work' on a ward is the satisfaction which people gain from giving care and keeping busy. The more independent the patient, the less the satisfaction from this point of view. Clarke found:

'Although they complained most about doing more than what they felt was a fair day's work, nurses were also concerned with having enough to do. Some nurses pointed out being kept busy as one of the advantages of working with older patients whom they could do things for. On the upgraded ward where there were fewer, less dependent patients than on the other long-stay wards and less administrative work to do than on the admission ward, there was sometimes a gap in the working day and some nurses felt bored or guilty. They found definition of day-to-day aims more of a problem than nurses on the long-stay wards who could see what they had to do and did it.'[14]

Thus while there is certainly a staffing level below which no one can be expected to give more than 'warehousing' care to patients it is clear that in less extreme circumstances depersonalising treatment will continue unless staff can be enabled to change what they define as 'work'. It is also essential that more senior nurses and other professionals should adjust their ideas about what 'nurses' work' properly consists of and so put less pressure on them to maintain an inflexible regime of orderliness, cleanliness and tidiness at the expense of independence and personal contact. The natural tendency of nurses to sit and chat together rather than 'really' mixing with patients also needs to be discouraged by senior staff.

Working conditions
Nevertheless, it is asking too much of human nature to provide active imaginative care if the working conditions are appalling and this is too often the case. A recent CHC report on conditions on the psychogeriatric wards of Fulbourn Hospital found that: 'The conditions in which the staff have to work are poor; the very heavy, difficult and thankless physical nursing which has to be done is made more burdensome by the lack of appropriate aids and the layout of old-fashioned buildings. Shortage of basic furnishing, a poor state of decoration and inadequate maintenance contribute to an air of neglect in some areas. Until recently one ward had to manage with too few dining-chairs and not enough cutlery, and badly torn wallpaper was said not to be due for replacement for another four years. '

Conditions in some of the toilets and bathrooms are described as 'little short of disgraceful'. Not only were there not enough toilets and baths for the number of patients, but these were also often a long way from the wards and they suffered from numerous other drawbacks, some of them easily and cheaply remedied. For example:

'— toilets (some new) that have doorways too narrow for a wheel-chair or walking frame, patient and nurse;
— no grab handles, built-up seats or other aids; toilet paper out of reach; no nurse call system;
— facilities used by both male and female patients;
— lack of privacy in toilets and baths;
— no lifting aids to help patients in and out of baths;
— medi-baths that do not work;
— no room round the bath for the staff to assist the patient;
— washing areas cramped and difficult for staff to use with non-mobile patients;
— inconveniently placed mirrors.

In a number of wards there was no sluice. Urinals, bed-pans and buckets used in washing the floors are cleaned out in the baths and washbasins. No one ward has the full range of the above problems, but every ward suffers from some of them.'

The report goes on to note that on a previous visit, CHC members had said:

'Incontinence presents an enormous problem to the sufferer and attendant alike, and is distressing to friends and relatives. To lay outsiders, it seems scandalous that nursing staff who are coping with incontinence continuously should not be provided with the most up-to-date equipment and facilities for dealing with it. We know that some improvements have been made, but even these seem not to have taken account of the size of the problem and the nature of geriatric nursing; much remains to be done.'[15]

There must be very many other hospitals where the same comments could be made.

It is true that many of the faults of these huge Victorian hospitals relate to their original design and their age, and there must always be a question as to how far it is wise to throw good money after bad by spending money on up-dating them. Nevertheless, relatively cheap attention to identifying priorities and making quick and clear decisions could prevent a great deal of frustration. For example, the St Augustine's enquiry found that:

'When a new Charge Nurse arrived on the ward in February, 1975, he found that they were having to use three old and rusty commodes which had been condemned for over a year. He joined in the attempts to get replacements, but was told that the Unit Administrator had marked the requisition "noted and deferred". The help of the Ward Medical Officer was again enlisted and after a great deal of persistent nagging, the commodes were eventually replaced more than 18 months after they had been condemned. The requisitioning system had no effective means of identifying priorities, and far too often those who sent in requisitions received no explanation for the failure to supply the items except that the requisition had been "noted and deferred". These words came to be treated with derision throughout the hospital.'[16]

Similarly, simple matters of maintenance can create problems out of all proportion to the time needed to deal with them. The CHC report on Fulbourn Hospital quoted above, found that it could take 6 weeks to get a light bulb replaced and over a half a year to get a medibath repaired. Repeated pleas to get an overflowing toilet repaired eventually produced a plumber—and then produced another one, two weeks later, to do the same job.

Responses of this kind (and again St Augustine's and Fulbourn are by no means unique, they are just better documented) indicate not only basic inefficiency, but also a contemptuous attitude to long-stay patients and those who care for them which is observable throughout the medical, nursing and administrative hierarchies and also in the public at large.

Conclusion

This chapter has shown how much *can* be done for long-term patients, so why do we not even take the trouble to use the resources which we have efficiently? If our nurses are capable of the quality of work described above, why are they not trained and encouraged to do it? Can we *really* not afford to repair lavatories or provide enough dining-room chairs or put in basic washing facilities? Given the will, a great deal can be done, but the will must come from the administrators, the policy makers and ultimately the general public, not just from the struggling medical and nursing staff concerned. There is a real and painful conflict between devoting resources to acute treatment and providing decent care for long-term patients. And as long-stay care loses out and becomes more and more third rate, the guilt we feel at poor provision becomes allied to the conviction that long-stay psychiatric hospital care is a last resort, to be avoided at all costs. Given this conviction, how can we genuinely respect those who staff this last resort? Society seems to be telling the staff of our long-stay wards 'Make us feel good by caring on our behalf', *but* 'Do not expect the resources to do it properly or social respect and prestige for doing it at all'.

What are the recipients of this message to make of it? They, like any human beings, value acknowledgement of their worth and pride in their job, so if they are to maintain their morale at all, they cannot but focus on the aspects of their work which make them feel better. Thus, the well-ordered routine, the beds all made by 9 am, the clean, tidy patients sitting neatly where they ought to sit, the sense of coping against the odds with under-staffing and out-of-date equipment and still producing 'good care'—these are the rewards. But to achieve such job satisfaction, the staff, like society at large, have to turn a deaf ear to another side of reality. If the patients are to be docile parts of a well-oiled machine, they cannot be seen as people—as individuals, clinging to vestiges of personality, choice, dignity and independence—as individuals who have lived long and full lives and have now lost the place in the community which gave them a role and identity—as individuals who are now living in 'social death'. So, the pain is buried in activity and routine; the patients are railroaded into passive conformity; and the message transmitted all too easily becomes 'We are caring for your body' *but* 'You, as a person, do not really exist'. If a new member of staff, fresh from training in 'good practice' or simply using her commonsense, tries to behave differently, she is only too likely to be quickly and firmly set on the path to conformity.

If we are to change this pattern, we need to bring into the open the competition for scarce resources between acute and chronic patients, and make *visible* decisions about the way the cake should be cut. Without this visibility, the weakest will always lose out. We need, as individuals and as a society, to become more honest about our ambivalent feelings. Yes, we feel concern for these patients, but we also feel guilt and anger about the responsibility which their existence lays upon us, and denial of these feelings is the seedbed of the 'double messages' described above. We need to bring the insights of social psychology into the management of our hospitals. As was noted at the beginning of this chapter, institutions have lives of their own and it is very hard to change their established habits. Even if good training, good staffing levels and up-to-date plant are provided, they will carry on as before unless change is very carefully engineered.[17] Above all, we need to be clear about our objectives in providing long-stay psychiatric care. At present, these objectives are often in conflict. The GP may consider that it is the role of the hospital to take a patient permanently off his hands as soon as he requests it. The residential home may think it is the hospital's job to cope with residents who are tiresome and difficult; the hospital may consider its role to be assessment, treatment or rehabilitation, after which it is the community's job to 'care'; the local press and public may consider that the main job of long-stay institutions is to keep people 'at risk' from physical harm, and so on. We cannot expect to achieve constructive reform unless we clarify our objectives—social, institutional, professional and personal—in providing long-stay care and continually monitor how far we are achieving them.

REFERENCES
1. David Jolley, All is not lost: new approaches to the management of old people with mental disorders in continuing care settings, *in* Molly Meacher (ed), *New methods of mental health care.* Pergamon Press, Oxford, 1979.
2. Ian Hanley et al., In touch with reality. *Social Work Today,* 12, 42, July 7 1981, 8–10.
3. K Conroy, Moorgreen Hospital, Southampton (unpublished paper).

4. Bev Savage et al., Improving the care of the elderly, *in* David Towell and Clive Harris (eds), *Innovation in patient care.* Croom Helm, London, 1979.

5. V Coulshed, A unitary approach to the care of the hospitalised elderly mentally ill. *British Journal of Social Work,* 10, 1, 1980, 19–32.

6. M Merchant and P Saxby, Reality orientation—a way forward. *Nursing Times,* 77, 33, August 12 1981, 1442–1445.

7. James T Leeming and Ann Luke, Multidisciplinary meetings with relatives of elderly hospital patients in continuing care wards. *Age and Ageing,* 6, 1, February 1977, 1–5.

8. Ronald Hamilton and Rita Simon, Art as a healer. *Geriatric Medicine,* 10, October 1980, 101–104.

9. B Richards, The team of experts. *Nursing Times,* 77, 34, August 19 1981, 1479–1480.

10. South East Thames Regional Health Authority. *Report of Committee of Enquiry, St Augustine's Hospital.* The Authority, Croydon, 1976.

11. C Godlove, L Richard and G Rodwell, *Time for Action.* Institute of Psychiatry, London, 1980.

12. May Clarke, *Working with elderly confused patients: nurses' expectations and experiences.* Department of Health and Social Security, London, 1974, (unpublished).

13. May Clarke, *The care of patients on a long-stay psychogeriatric ward.* Department of Health and Social Security, London, 1974, (unpublished).

14. See ref. 12.

15. Cambridge Community Health Council, *Report of members' visits to the geriatric wards at Fulbourn Hospital in February/March 1981.* Cambridge CHC, Cambridge, 1981.

16. See ref. 10.

17. E J Miller, Autonomy, dependency and organisation change, *in* David Towell and Clive Harris (eds), *Innovation in patient care.* Croom Helm, London, 1979.

8 Residential caring

It is well known that the original purpose of local authority residential care, as proposed by Aneurin Bevan and set out under Part III of the National Assistance Act 1948, was to provide a life free from anxiety or responsibility for retired people who, while they might be 'in need of care and attention', were not envisaged as being too disabled to undertake basic self-care. Indeed the early image was the reverse—they could well be active and independent and enter a home simply to receive a well-deserved rest. Bevan's 'hotel' concept never materialised in the form in which he intended but its ghost lingers on to bedevil the official image of what residential care should be, what it should do, how it should be staffed and whom it should serve. Almost everywhere the theory of the criterion 'capable of self care' has given way in practice—from moderate concessions about 'needing some assistance' or 'occasional incontinence' on the one hand, to outright acceptance of care for the bedfast, the terminally ill and the severely-demented on the other. But the point at which the line is drawn depends in many cases, not on a carefully-worked out assessment of the weight of dependence, nor on a clear-cut definition of the objectives of residential care, but on variables such as availability of long-term psychogeriatric hospital beds in a particular area; the personal attitudes of officers in charge; the availability and nature of sheltered housing; the adequacy of geriatric and psychogeriatric assessment and treatment facilities; and the quality and quantity of domiciliary support services. If it was clear and agreed what purpose residential homes should serve, it would be possible to make some attempt to map out the staffing, the support services and the range of specialist provision required and see where facilities needed to be improved or resources shifted. Without clear and realistic objectives, the *ad hoc* muddle and the resentment of those running homes who feel unjustly overburdened and understaffed will continue.

The situation is no clearer in the voluntary and private sector. Here committees or proprietors are perhaps more justified in saying, as many have done, 'this particular institution has not been set up to cope with severe disability and while we may try to 'care to the end' if disablement develops after admission, we will not admit those who are already disabled or continue to care if we feel that the burden is too great'. Legally, they are quite right. If 'nursing care' (whatever that may mean) is to be provided, the law says it must be provided in NHS hospitals, or in private nursing homes which have a separate legal status and which are registered and inspected by officials of the National Health Service. Thus a private or voluntary home may *in fact* 'care to the end' but if it states in its brochure that it provides nursing care it will find itself required to change its status or to seek dual registration.

Human needs cannot be controlled by parliamentary draughtsmen however. In practice the reluctance of people to enter care until they really cannot look after themselves or are beyond the care of relatives; the sheer pressure of demand; the difficulty of finding a hospital-based alternative; and the very high cost of private nursing home care are forcing the non-statutory sector to take increasing responsibility for the mentally and physically disabled. Thus in both the statutory and non-statutory sectors, residential homes are in the position of purporting to do one thing and actually doing something quite different—with the result that staff levels, training, design of buildings, assessment techniques and care and rehabilitation skills are all too often inadequate for the work to be done.

Incidence of mental disability in residential homes

There has been much discussion, particularly following the publication of Meacher's *Taken for a ride*, of the advantages and disadvantages of segregating the 'confused' and 'alert' elderly, and this issue is dealt with more fully below. To some extent, however, it is now an academic argument. It is true that specialist homes may still be set up, but *all* homes, at least in the statutory sector, are now likely to have some residents with dementia or other mental disabilities and in many cases both the severity of the disability and the proportion of mentally-disabled residents will be high. Thus the Office of Health Economics quotes Jefferys as estimating that in 1978 for every two elderly confused patients in psychiatric hospitals there were a further four in residential homes. Arie is also quoted as estimating that between one-third and one-half of residents in homes 'are appreciably demented'.[1] These estimates have been borne out by such statistics as are available and by detailed local studies such as those undertaken by Wilkin and his colleagues in Manchester[2] and by Gilleard, Pattie and Dearman in Yorkshire.[3] Such global estimates do not tell the whole story of course. Within one local authority, the level of mental disability is likely to vary considerably from one home to another, depending on the attitudes of the officers in charge, physical facilities, staffing policy and the sheer accident of the speed and nature of individual deterioration. If several residents develop severe disability or difficult behavioural problems at the same time, a home which may have been coping quite well is likely to become overwhelmed. Overall, however, there is no doubt that, regardless of official policy, the proportion of dementia sufferers in old peoples' homes is already high and is on the increase. Moreover, there is ample evidence that while psychogeriatric hospitals have a higher *average* level of severity of dementia sufferers, some of the residents being cared for in homes are just as severely impaired as those in hospital.

At the time of writing the proportion of dementia sufferers in residential care is still a minority but there is no guarantee that this will continue to be the case. Gilleard et al. conclude from comparing data over a 10 year period that: 'there has been a continuing increase in the size of this 'minority' within the social services homes for the elderly and extrapolation of this trend might lead to a prediction that this 'minority' will in the near future become a majority, with serious implications for future plans for the care and management of old people'.[4] These are *facts* which will not go away and it is high time we took their implications into proper account.

Mixing 'alert' and 'confused' residents
Although all local authority homes are likely to be 'mixed' to some extent it is still worth considering how this 'mix' can best be managed and whether some specialist homes for the most severely mentally disabled should be provided.

Wilkin and his colleagues ('the Manchester team') in their very detailed research report on 'mixed' homes conclude that by a very rough rule of thumb, 30% of residents with mental impairment can be coped with without too damaging an effect on the regime in the home or the quality of life of alert residents.[5] CPA in one of its Homes Advice Broadsheets suggests 25% as the ideal limit,[6] but that is in the voluntary and private sector where staffing levels and purpose built facilities are even less likely to be available than in the statutory sector. However, as the Manchester team point out, simple measurement of levels of impairment and dependency and behavioural disturbance are not the only factors to be taken into account in calculating a reasonable balance. Levels of physical disability and dependency, physical environment, staffing levels and other considerations such as average age, sex and social class will all affect the issue. Some homes practice *internal* segregation—by providing a specialist floor or wing—in the belief that this enables staff to be deployed where they are most needed and also enables an appropriate regime to be established for the most confused, without cutting them off from general social activities. Other officers in charge resist this on the ground that it is too easy for a specialist wing to be regarded as punitive and its residents as 'no-hopers'; there may also be concern that the quality of care administered cannot be properly supervised. Certainly the Manchester team come out firmly with the view that, in the homes they studied, internal segregation did not produce 'any substantial improvement in the quality of life experienced by residents, either for the lucid and able or for the confused and physically disabled'. They found that integration could produce mutual assistance and a more lively atmosphere as well as being less potentially damaging for the severely disabled and possibly a more cost-effective use of resources.[7]

It is often assumed that segregation protects lucid residents from being distressed by confused ones, but this is not necessarily so. The Manchester team found that 55% of the staff whom they interviewed thought it was confused residents who needed protection from harassment by lucid people and 60% felt that it was not the confused residents but those who presented personality problems who were most difficult to cope with. Forty-one per cent of care staff found the confused residents the easiest to care for and 71% said that they liked working with the confused. Most important of all, perhaps, was the relationship which seemed to exist between activity levels and tolerance. Staff widely attributed friction between residents to boredom, and more than 60% of the residents said that they had little or nothing with which to occupy their time. It seems clear that coping with a 'mix' of residents is much more a matter of good general management than a question of labelling, and then segregating, 'reject' residents.[8]

There is however no doubt that a degree of informal 'self-segregation' occurs frequently and it may be encouraged, consciously or unconsciously, by staff. For example a study of the architectural design implications of residential homes for old people by Lipman and Slater found that in all eight purpose-built homes of various designs which they studied, the residents had become segregated according to sex, mental designation and degree of continence (the confused often being put in separate lounges or in larger bedrooms) and there was little interaction between rational and confused residents.[9]

'Specialist' homes
But what of specialist homes which only admit residents who are diagnosed as suffering from severe dementia or other mental disability of an equally disabling nature? Enid Levin, in an unpublished

report written for CPA, gives the following account of the development of this facility.

'Specialist homes for the mentally infirm first developed in the fifties and sixties, against the background, not only of the 1948 National Assistance Act, but also the 1959 Mental Health Act, with its emphasis on care in the community. Another factor was the policy of closing the former Public Assistance Institutions. These had contained a large number of confused elderly people whose needs had to be catered for at a time when long-term psychiatric hospital beds were being run down and yet no-one wanted to challenge the 'hotel concept' of Part III accommodation. By 1966, 37 authorities (25%) already possessed a unit or units exclusively or largely for the elderly mentally infirm. In addition, 43% of local authorities had plans to provide such accommodation in the future (about half of these had some specialised provision already). Thus in all 56 authorities either had specialist homes or proposed to set them up. Some of these plans do not seem to have materialised, however. A DHSS list obtained in 1976 showed that in England alone 42 local authorities were providing 71 specialist homes.'

Since then relatively few new specialist homes have been opened and doubts about the validity of the concept have increased. It is argued that such homes are in danger of becoming 'dumping grounds' not only for those with severe dementia and accompanying behavioural disorder but also for those with difficult personality problems as well as the elderly mentally handicapped and other social rejects. It is suggested that it is difficult to maintain adequate staff and an active environment in such segregated homes and that once 'labelled' by such segregation a resident is likely to have all her wishes and behaviour treated as invalid. Here are two short examples from Meacher's study of three specialist and three ordinary homes *Taken for a ride*.[10]

'A woman of 88 who was disoriented, tangential in speech and subject to excessive fiddling complained at the time of my visit of sharp pains in her back. The staff were openly suspicious of the reality of this alleged indisposition and assured her somewhat flippantly that she would soon be better. At her interview she protested bitterly at this indifference. "I wish the doctor would come—pain in my back and all over. I want to go somewhere where somebody knows more about my back. My back is a misery. I'd like a change now. I'd like to go to Furleigh Hospital and see what they can do!"' Despite her pleas and periodical groaning the matron did not finally call the doctor until several days had elapsed.'

Another resident who had been diagnosed as suffering from 'senile psychosis' and whose symptoms were not sufficiently severe for her to score as confused on Meacher's scale complained:

'There's nothing to do. They've got maids to do it all. You're not allowed to help anyone infirm or old, like Mrs Guthrie. . . You're free to a certain extent, but I must say that going out to tea once I didn't tell them and they nearly called the police. And they wanted to wash a dress of mine, but it's always been dry-cleaned, so I didn't let them wash it, as it would have shrunk, and I have lost six blouses—don't know where they've gone. And another thing I don't like is that the keys are taken away and you can't lock the doors. How they talk to me if you do anything wrong. One or two of them are nice, but they seem to order one about. All nice in a certain way if you do what they want. But I don't see much of them. They seem to rule the place, no doubt about that. I don't like it when you have to do what you're told.'

Meacher's work has been interpreted as coming down against specialisation but in fact he warns against its dangers, and especially inadequate selection of residents and insufficient or untrained staff, rather than against specialisation in principle. Indeed, there seems to be little doubt that given a real and positive interest and investment from the local authority plus adequate back up from the psychogeriatrician and CPN, specialist homes can provide a more lively and more relaxed environment than more traditional establishments. For example Newcastle upon Tyne runs five specialist homes in very close co-operation with the psychogeriatric service at the Brighton Clinic (see p. 47). All prospective residents are carefully assessed at the clinic and staff can call for help or advice on management at any time. Staffing levels take account of the high level of dependency. Almost all residents have their own rooms. Perhaps it is significant that the Newcastle specialist homes are run by the mental health section of social services and not by the section dealing with residential care for the elderly. The model is thus that of a hostel for the mentally ill and the staff in charge have their expertise in that field. The result appears to be a much greater emphasis on communication with residents and encouraging interaction and activity than is commonly found in standard old people's homes.

Another specialist home, 'Woodside' in Birmingham, is run on a system which is deliberately adapted to the needs of the really severely-demented resident who has virtually no short-term memory. The regime is based on the premise that the home is there to meet the needs of the residents and not vice versa. Meals are provided at fixed times but residents can eat how and when they wish if they are unwilling to come to the dining room. No night sedation is given. If residents want to wander all night they are free to do so. Formal reality orientation is thought to be too much of a strain and to produce agitation and aggression, but staff are taught to be aware of exactly what residents can or cannot do and a 'key worker' is assigned on the basis of one worker to about three residents to give individual care and to observe and report at regular staff meetings how the resident is progressing and any incident of interest or achievement. Two-hourly toiletting keeps incontinence to a minimum.

Staff maintain that this regime, when offered to people who have virtually no short-term memory, enables them to be coped with in a happy relaxed way which makes the home pleasurable to work in. Aggression is very rare because there is no frustration; relations between staff and residents become close and trusting; domestics share in the care task, at the expense of their own work if necessary, and especially at evenings and weekends; staff turnover is very low indeed. The basic philosophy is that the home is run as the residents need it, not as society thinks they ought to have it. Taking this to its logical conclusion can appear shocking at first sight. All residents have their own rooms, for example, but they are minimally furnished and impersonal. If a resident goes to sleep in the wrong one, the rightful occupant will be steered elsewhere. Most residents are 'gatherers' and 'strippers', so personal possessions have to be discouraged; they simply could not be prevented from getting lost or damaged. Clothing and washing things are centrally stored; there are no handbags. This means that the staff do not have to worry about inessentials and can concentrate on what really matters which they believe is building up trusting relationships and creating a real home where residents' confusion is not compounded by the unnecessary demands of social conventions. The staff can, they say, cope with any level of mental disability and only seek hospital admission in very rare cases of persistent or serious violence to other residents, or if there is serious physical illness. However, they do enjoy double the normal staff ratio and two waking night staff are always on duty. It must also be emphasised that a regime of this kind demands very careful selection of residents. It is suitable only for people who really have a virtually total loss of short-term memory and orientation. Less severely demented residents would find it destructive and distressing.

In summary, there would seem to be quite a good case for 'specialist' homes *provided* their purpose, their regime, their staff levels and staff training, their psychogeriatric and social services back-up, and their selection processes are carefully thought through. Inadequacy in any of these aspects can lead to a home becoming the worst sort of dumping ground and providing the worst sort of care. But even if the number of specialist homes increases, ordinary homes will still have to care for a large proportion of demented and otherwise mentally-disabled old people and they must be enabled to do the job properly.

Clarifying responsibility for care
The first essential, as was stated in the opening paragraph of this chapter, is for the DHSS and the local authorities to make a clear *administrative and political* decision that long-term hospital care should only be considered for those who, in the words of a working party report by the special interest group of the Royal College of Psychiatrists, are suffering from:

(a) incontinence uncontrolled by regular toiletting and other treatment
(b) serious immobility
(c) gross dementia—of a degree which prevents the person from taking part in social activities or significantly appreciating his surroundings
(d) severe and unmanageable behavioural disturbance
(e) mental illness of a kind which requires on-going skilled management.

If that could be agreed, we could concentrate our minds on the necessary action to make it practicable.

Clarifying the role of care staff
There can be few occupations in which the job which staff are trained and paid to do and the job which actually needs to be done differ so widely. Are care staff as their status as manual workers, and their frequent lack of any but the most basic training suggest, slightly superior domestics whose job includes the washing and feeding of bodies as well as the making of beds? Or are they substitute family members for whom the mental well-being and independence of resi-

dents is just as important as their physical health? Are they running homes or 'warehouses'? Inevitably, untrained staff whose only relevant experience of giving care is likely to be with young children, and whose expectation of a working task is physical labour, will at best infantilise and overprotect residents, and at worst treat them as bodies and not people, unless they are given another perspective by which to judge their role. This was well brought out by May Clarke in her description of the way in which nurse assistants on a long-stay psychogeriatric ward viewed their task (see pp. 99–100), but it is equally true of residential homes. Exactly the same task can change its nature radically if the objective of the staff member concerned becomes different. The Manchester team illustrate this by contrasting some of the bath sessions which they observed. In some, the greatest care was taken to make the process enjoyable for the resident. In others, baths were 'little more than a cleaning operation performed in a perfunctory manner with little or no social intercourse and on occasion scant concern for physical comfort'. Both types of bathing took almost exactly the same time. The authors emphasise the importance of encouraging staff to consider not only the objective purpose of a task such as bathing but its subjective meaning for residents 'as a social event; as an opportunity for the resident to exercise autonomy and self care; as a means of promoting physical rehabilitation or simply as a period of relaxation for the resident. . . A wider definition such as this inevitably requires staff to approach the bathing with a rather different set of criteria by which to measure their own practice; the extent to which the resident is cleaner becomes a relatively minor consideration.'[11] The same is true of any activity (eating, bedmaking, dressing, gardening, housework, washing up or cooking for example) in which residents are or could be involved.

If staff (including officers in charge and seniors in the social services department) are to change their definition of the nature of the task, there must, as we have already seen in the nursing setting, be a radical shift in *external* expectation of role from the social services committee, the relatives, the press and the general public as well as a skilled transfer of self-critical responsibility *within* the homes. As Liz Ward puts it:

'Enabling residents to be better off for their period in care, (whether children or adults, whether their handicap is social, physical or mental), depends on certain key factors. There has to be a diminishing of the importance of the hierarchy, and there has to be a flexibility of routine. Open communication needs to be worked for, so that people have time to talk to each other, and above all, to listen to what is being said. Objectives that are realistic enough, and specific enough to be achieved need to be shared and understood, not only within the resident group, but across the boundaries to include colleagues in the community. However special the residential environment, involvement across the boundaries is crucial in enabling residents to maximise independence and develop personal coping skills.

Taken together, these key factors represent the nux of residential intervention. They add up to a process of simply being in touch with each other. Simple, and yet seemingly so difficult to achieve especially so if we are too busy to give ourselves time.'[12]

Changing the job description of care staff
This is, of course, all very well. But the staff may be untrained manual workers who do not want the responsibility of looking at their job in any other way. And a very high level of physical and mental dependency may make it genuinely almost impossible to set aside and maintain time for staff training and focused discussion on residents' needs. What then? One approach, which current unemployment of educated and trained people may make easier to implement, is to accept that the work of care staff *is* skilled and recruit and pay them accordingly. For example, a home in Ealing is run by eight basic grade social workers with an experienced residential social worker as officer in charge and an experienced nurse as deputy. We are told that:

'Many traditional aspects of care for the elderly were openly thrown out or discreetly ignored. First, recruitment of staff moved away from the "nice little job" image of the usual care assistant. A career structure akin to that of residential social work with children was implemented. Staff tended to be young and wishing to gain experience before undertaking social work or nursing training. Recruiting of domestic staff was also carefully undertaken. Those who expected just to push a broom were not offered jobs, while those who expressed a willingness to be involved with residents and the home were actively encouraged!'[13]

It is difficult to imagine a better training for a field social worker than time spent finding out what 'caring' means in practice, what the problems of residential care staff are, and how disabled and demented elderly people should be looked after. Is it too Utopian to *expect* that applicants for a CQSW course should have spent a year working in a residential care setting? Or that at least one member of the senior staff should have a CSS or CQSW qualification and have had some experience in field social work?

Staffing levels

It is of course not only the quality of staffing which is important, but the need to maintain a level of staffing which is sufficient to meet the dependency needs in any particular home. It is essential that local authorities should maintain a *constant* monitoring of levels of dependency and be prepared to alter staffing ratios and admission policy accordingly. The Manchester team illustrated this graphically with the use of a modified version of the Crichton Royal Behavioural Rating Scale (CRBRS) which was originally developed by R A Robinson in 1968.[14] Their version has 10 items; mobility, memory, orientation, communication, co-operation, restlessness, dressing, feeding, bathing and continence. Each item is rated between 0 (no problems) and 4 (severe problems), except for memory and feeding which are rated between 0 and 3. The minimum possible score for any individual is therefore 0 and the maximum 38. An Officer in Charge, who is accustomed to the scale, can assess each resident and thus make a fairly accurate gauge of the overall level of disability with which her staff are coping. The importance of this is clearly illustrated by the Manchester team when they calculated the staff time needed to bath, dress and toilet disabled residents. With regard to toiletting, for example, the team were advised that if the regime was to attempt to reintroduce bowel and bladder control and not just be a cleaning up operation, incontinent people need to be taken to the toilet *at least* 5 times a day. They found by observation that residents with a score of more than 10 on the CRBRS scale were likely to need this help, and that each occasion took an average 5·5 minutes of staff time. To provide care at this level, 3 of the 6 homes which they studied would need more than 30% more staff. The smallest increase required was 12·5% and that was in the home with the lowest proportion of disabled people. Similar estimates can be made for activities such as dressing and bathing for which residents with a CRBRS score of over 10 are also likely to need help, and, of course, the higher the score the more staff time is likely to be required (this may cease to be true when the disability is so severe that the staff give up trying). Understaffing means that, willy-nilly, residents are left sitting in their urine and faeces and that care is provided on an impersonal 'conveyor belt' system with a disregard of privacy and dignity and with residents being left half-dressed or sitting on a lavatory, while another one is being attended to. It also means very early hours for dressing and undressing, so that some residents have to be dressed at 6 am to enable all residents to be ready for breakfast by 8.30 am, and some residents are got ready for bed at 6 pm so that the burden on night staff is reduced. 'Frills' like talking to residents, encouraging independence and activity and reinforcing reality go by the board, and the symptoms of depression and dementia are inevitably exacerbated.[15]

Staff support

It is one thing to know the level of dependency which staff are coping with and quite another to do something about it. What action can, realistically, be taken? There seem to be three approaches which need to be used simultaneously.

1. The mobilisation of specialist (and often hospital-based) social workers, physiotherapists, occupational therapists, geriatric and psychogeriatric nurses, geriatricians and psychiatrists to give regular and 'at call' support and training to residential staff. These skills, are, as the Manchester team have pointed out, far too precious to be hoarded in a hospital setting and residential homes make an ideal base from which they can be made available in the community.[16]

2. Creation of an honest working relationship between hospital and home. If psychiatrists expect homes to accept their patients for long stay care, homes must be confident that they will take them back in an emergency or if dependency really does become too great for residential care staff to cope with, and perhaps also for relief or day care. If this assurance is given, and adhered to, homes, like relatives, are much more willing to go on coping. For example, Margo et al. found that out of 100 referrals to the Oxford psychogeriatric service from old people's homes during 1972–78 only nine became long stay hospital patients and only a minority required admission at all.[17] In Hereford, D M D White found that it made a major difference when he gave 5 of his 20 relief beds to the staff of local authority homes for use at *their* discretion. It relieved their sense of impotence; it provided an opportunity for senior staff in homes to compare notes and decide who most needed relief and it brought hospital and residential care staff into close contact at hospital case conferences.

3. Operate a flexible staffing policy. This is of course easier said than done but it should be possible to deploy back-up peripatetic staff in a particular area not only to meet crises caused by sickness and holidays but also temporary high levels of dependency (such staff would need exceptional training and status). It should also be pos-

sible, as the Manchester team suggest, to explore the feasibility of providing extra NHS staff to deal with temporary increases in the burden of care. This would, after all, be a much cheaper alternative to admitting a patient to a long-stay hospital bed.

4. Monitor existing dependency levels before accepting new residents. This may be more practicable in an area like Manchester which is relatively well provided with Part III homes but it is important that social service departments should take *informed* decisions on this matter, using the CRBRS rating scales referred to above.

One example of what *can* be done is provided by an experimental 'joint high dependency home' in Stockport. This facility has four senior staff and nearly double the usual number of care staff. Some of the senior staff have a nursing background and support is available from a senior nursing officer. The Health Authority pays a GP for three sessions a week, one of which is spent with the geriatrician in the hospital, one doing 'rounds' in the home and one is used to pay for on-call responsibilities. A part-time physiotherapist is provided from the hospital and additional OT activities are planned. Additional facilities such as bathing aids, variable-height beds and waste-disposal units lessen the physical strain on care staff. Admission is controlled by a small panel led by the geriatrician and a senior community social worker. The home is planned to offer 'three main environments: the personal where the resident can have complete privacy, perhaps best supplied by a bedsitting room with adjacent toilet; a restricted environment, itself split into selective and non-selective areas, where residents can dine and relax in small groups; and the extended environment arranged for those who wish to take part in specific activities'. It will, as Stockport's Assistant SSD Director wryly says 'not conform to the DHSS building notes and will be markedly different from those buildings which have been based on the historical evolution of styles of caring'.[18] Purpose-built homes of this quality are obviously a rare luxury in today's hard times but the Stockport project offers a goal towards which we can work and an indication of how, even in less ideal surroundings, it can be achieved.

Conclusion
This chapter has focused on the administrative decisions which need to be made by those responsible for residential care, rather than on ways in which homes can defend the mental health of their residents. CPA has spelled out in other publications[19] the key importance of

thorough pre-admission assessment—physical, psychiatric and social; careful planning of the admission process; maintaining personal identity and responsibility; promoting continence; creating a supportive atmosphere; keeping contact with family and friends, and so on. Much of the material in this report relating to long-term nursing care and group therapy is also relevant. We know a great deal about what *can* be done and in a few places it *is* being done. But it is no use willing the end without willing the means, and the means in CPA's view will not be made available until we have:

1. A clear acceptance of responsibility by the residential sector for the care of both mentally and physically disabled elderly people unless they have some characteristic which clearly demands hospital care.
2. The provision by the National Health Service of resources, expertise and support to enable this responsibility to be properly carried.
3. A mandatory system of supplementation of approved fees in the voluntary and private sector so that old people whose need for residential care is acknowledged and whose income is insufficient to pay for it can also be offered proper care in non-statutory homes.
4. Willingness in both the statutory and non-statutory sectors to recognise that residential work with the elderly is a demanding and skilled task with great potential in the development of community services and that staff should receive the training, status and pay appropriate to their work.

REFERENCES
1. Office of Health Economics, *Dementia in old age*. OHE, London, 1979.
2. G Evans, B Hughes, D Wilkin with D Jolley, *The management of mental and physical impairment in non-specialist residential homes for the elderly.* University Hospital of South Manchester, Psychogeriatric Unit, Research Section, Manchester, 1981.
3. C J Gilleard, A H Pattie and D G Dearman, Behavioural disabilities in psychogeriatric patients and residents in old people's homes. *Journal of Epidemiology and Community Health*, 34, 2, June 1980, 106–110.
4. *ibid.*
5. See ref. 2.
6. Alison Norman, *Mental health and illness in old people's homes.* Centre for Policy on Ageing, London, 1980. (Homes Advice Broadsheets 6).
7. See ref. 2.
8. *ibid.*
9. Robert Slater and Alan Lipman, Staff assessments on confusion and the situation of confused residents in homes for old people. *The Gerontologist*, 17, 6, 1977, 523–530.

120

10. Michael Meacher, *Taken for a ride: special residential homes for confused elderly people: a study of separation in social policy.* Longman Group, London, 1972.
11. See ref. 2.
12. Liz Ward, There just isn't time. *Social Work Today,* 11, 1, September 4 1979, 21.
13. B D Austin, Care without caring: looking after the elderly in residential homes. *Nursing Times,* 77, 5, January 29 1981, 203–204.
14. R A Robinson, The assessment centre, *in* J G Howells (ed), *Modern perspectives in the psychiatry of old age,* Brunner, Mazel, New York, no date.
15. See ref. 2.
16. David Wilkin and David Jolley, *Behavioural problems among old people in geriatric wards, psychogeriatric wards and residential homes 1976–1978.* University Hospital of South Manchester, Psychogeriatric Unit, Research Section, Manchester 1979.
17. J L Margo, J R Robinson and S Corea, Referrals to a psychiatric service from old people's homes. *British Journal of Psychiatry,* 136, April 1980, 396–401.
18. R J Lewis, Is this home the place for the very frail elderly? *Geriatric Medicine,* April 1979, 17–18.
19. Alison J Norman, *Rights and risk: a discussion document on civil liberty in old age.* CPA, London, 1979, and Alison J Norman, *Mental health and illness in old people's homes.* CPA, London 1980. (Homes Advice Broadsheet 6).

9 Meeting the challenge

This report has illustrated the wide range of treatment and support which is potentially available to mentally-ill older people. It has sought to demonstrate that far from the cause being hopeless or the pit bottomless, this is a field in which a reasonable injection of skill, optimism, determination and funding can provide a positive and viable service. It has described the potential of the primary care services, both statutory and voluntary, for providing imaginative tailor-made 'care packages'; the ability of well-organised and well-led psychogeriatric service teams to back up the primary carers with specialist skills and readily available assessment and treatment; the value of the community psychiatric nurse (CPN) in bridging the barrier between the hospital and the community, mobilising voluntary support services and backing up caring neighbours and relatives; the high quality of service which can be offered by day hospitals and centres, and by properly staffed and equipped residential homes; and the great potential of nurses in improving the quality of long-stay hospital care.

And yet it must be admitted that this wide range of potential treatment and support has to be set against the background of national economic recession and health and social services crisis—a background of short-term, short-sighted economies and desperate infighting for such financial resources as are available. While this report was being written, Enfield Health District said categorically that it could not provide any service at all for psychogeriatric admissions because it could not afford to staff the necessary beds, and the Enfield case is probably unusual in having caught the public attention rather than being exceptional in itself. Vital local services, such as home help, are being rationed by making charges and cutting hours and staff; residential homes being closed and grants to voluntary services cut; the National Health Service, already rocking under the impact of competition from private medicine, is launching itself into a re-organisation which will multiply the difficulties of developing joint planning between health and social services. How, in the face of all this, can we expect to mobilise energies which will make the provision of good treatment and care for older people with mental illness the rule rather than exception?

It sounds almost impossible and yet, paradoxically, the need to make more efficient use of resources, combined with the opportunity for starting afresh in the new District Health Authorities could provide the impetus for major improvement in the quality of psychogeriatric service delivery.

Already there are many signs of earlier and less crisis-oriented assessment of need through improved co-operation between social services and other primary care workers, and assessment before admission to the waiting list for residential care is also being done more carefully. The training and status of home helps and residential care assistants is beginning to improve, and the opportunity for geriatric and psychogeriatric experience in basic and post qualification training of nurses, doctors, social workers and other professionals is better than it was, though still often very inadequate. These are moves in the right direction which can and should be vigorously pursued. More specifically, the NHS re-organisation will give an opportunity to the new Health Districts to implement the recommendations of the Nodder Report[1] on the establishment of a Psychiatric Service Management Team (PSMT) in each District to be responsible to the District Management Team (DMT) for the overall planning of a comprehensive psychiatric service and with control over its own budget. Apart from administrative, nursing, medical, finance and other professional health service representatives, the PSMT would have senior representatives from the social services department (or departments) with full 'member' status. The team's task would be to create properly planned and integrated hospital, day hospital and CPN services in relationship with primary care workers and the social services departments. Planning the care and treatment of the elderly would obviously be a major part of this task.

The Nodder Report recommends that the PSMT's role in this respect would be:

i to identify, in conjunction with those responsible for geriatric services and with those responsible for local authority services in the district, the range and nature of the psychiatric support which those services need;

ii to ensure the provision of assessment and re-assessment facilities for elderly psychiatric patients in general hospitals;

iii to draw up, in conjunction with those responsible for geriatric and local authority services, admission policies and criteria for avoiding misplacement; and policies for correcting misplacement where it occurs as between these different services;

iv to identify the nurse and other staffing levels essential for an adequate psychiatric service to the District and to initiate recruitment and training programmes aimed at achieving these;

v to ensure that the psychiatric services to the District operate as an entity, and that there are arrangements for internally transferring any patients initially misplaced as between individual elements of the psychiatric service;

vi to see that services are organised with the aim of achieving an acceptable balance of work between the mental illness hospital and the psychiatric unit in the general hospitals, with facilities for staff rotation where desired;

vii to foster the development of teams specially concerned with services for elderly psychiatric patients;

viii to develop training for such services;

ix to set standards and targets aimed at improving performance, and the quality of life for elderly psychiatric patients needing long-term care;

x to monitor progress in achieving these standards and targets.

If these responsibilities were taken seriously in all Health Districts, the provision of psychogeriatric care and treatment would indeed be transformed.

One key aspect in the planning of service delivery in the new Districts is the role of the big mental illness hospitals. There is a grave danger that, while acute services of all kinds may move with comparative ease into the Districts, long-stay care will remain isolated in the old mental hospitals with all the attendant dangers which were described in Chapter 7. The population of 'old' long-stay patients in these hospitals (patients admitted before 1971) is expected by the DHSS to decline by death or discharge at a rate of between 9% and 12% up to 1991,[2] but there is a very real risk that sheer pressure of demand will result in long-stay wards being filled up with demented elderly people for whom there is just nowhere else to go. As we know from the epidemiological and demographic factors outlined in the first chapter of this report, the demand for 24 hour care is likely to rise inexorably until after the end of the century and the number of available places, whether in hospital or residential homes, already falls far short of what on any reasonable estimate is needed. Indeed, Arie takes the view that the under-provision of residential care facilities is the biggest pitfall for the future of psychogeriatrics and that the pressure building up as a result will have repercussions on the whole National Health Service.[3] It is vital that this pressure should be met by the provision of properly staffed residential homes and by localised hospital units which are integrated with day care, relief care and the other psychogeriatric services. The chance must not be lost to close these

Victorian relics and transfer their resources to District-based and joint-funded amenities.

Any discussion of future health service provision inevitably raises what Sir Ronald Gibson has called 'the awful separation' of the health services from the social services. Some people see the abolition of Area Health Authorities which, in many cases, had coterminous boundaries with social services, as the *coup de grace* for the development of joint-care planning and shared responsibility. How, they ask, can social services possibly spare sufficient senior officer time to develop any really effective collaboration with perhaps half a dozen Districts? And how can SSD representatives operate effectively as members of a PSMT which has across-the-board responsibility for psychiatric services when responsibility in their own Department is split vertically between residential, day care and domiciliary services? Other observers argue that health and social services are, in any case, so disparate in structure, accountability, funding and basic priorities that 'coterminosity' of boundaries is a cosmetic irrelevance which has only disguised the real problems. But all would agree that there are no easy answers. Even the Nodder Report can do no more than list the difficulties and express the hope that inter-disciplinary initiatives in joint working, joint learning experience and joint training will reduce some of the tension and provide closer links. However, necessity is the mother of invention, and as the pressures increase it seems probable that joint planning and shared service provision will become inescapable. It is likely that this will develop through localised and face-to-face co-operation with relatively small joint funded projects such as day care, increased health service input into residential care, involvement of CPNs in voluntary and social service provision and deliberate deployment of the psychogeriatric team in the community along the lines suggested by Jefferys (see p. 53). But such innovative and collaborative services cannot exist in a vacuum. To be effective they need to be set up as part of a *strategy* for shared caring which looks at need first and then looks at ways in which resources can be moved round or mobilised to meet that need. Localised initiative from below should stimulate strategic planning at all levels of policy making and itself be fostered by such planning. There must be a real desire to make things work from the Government, the DHSS, and the health services at Regional level as well as from local authorities and Health Districts. The basic necessity is the will to succeed and confidence, based on growing experience, that we can succeed. We can no longer plead ignorance or helplessness. If we do not now provide adequate treatment and care for older people with mental disability, it is because we, as a society, deliberately choose not to do so—a decision which we as individuals may one day bitterly regret.

REFERENCES
1. *Organisation and management problems of mental illness hospitals,* Report of a Working Group, DHSS, London, 1980.
2. *The provision of in-patient facilities for the mentally ill—a paper to assist NHS planners.* DHSS, London, 1981.
3. Personal communication.

Appendix 1
DOMICILIARY ASSESSMENT FORMS IN USE AT MOORGREEN HOSPITAL, SOUTHAMPTON*

SURNAME   CASE NOTE NO.   OTHER HOSP. NO.

SURNAME		CASE NOTE NO. OTHER HOSP. NO.
Forenames		Date first referred
Marital status:	S. M.	Sep. Div. Wid. Date first seen
Date of birth		Age at first referral Religion
Referred by		Where seen
Address		Name & address of relatives or friends
1.		1.
2.		2.
3.		3.
4.		4.

GP
SSD Team	Social worker
Psychiatric health visitor	
Health visitor	Home nurse
Geriatrician	Other specialist
Home help	Meals on wheels
Other workers involved	

Family history
  Mental illness
  Background

Personal history
Birthplace	Schooling
Job	Retirement age
Husband's job	

Marriage
Present status	Previous marriages
Harmony	Health of spouse

Home
Type of dwelling	Tenancy
State of home	Toilet facilities
Suitability of home	Bed upstairs/
	downstairs
	Hot water
	Heating
	Type of cooker

Support
Spouse	Financial assets
Children	
Neighbours	
Others	

*Reprinted by permission of Dr Colin Godber, Moorgreen Hospital

Physical health
General health
Chest pain/breathlessness
Abdo loss of weight/appetite/Bor/blood
CNS blackouts/headaches
GUS dysuria/incontinence
Previous illnesses

Examination of patient

Mental state	*Dysphasia*
Appearance/dressing	Pen
State of hygiene	Watch
	Button
Conscious level (drowsy, alert)	R/L orientation
Vision/hearing	Body agnosia knee
	nose
	elbow
Speech	Sensory inattention

Mood (eg euphoria, depressed, v depressed)
Concentration
Psychomotor activity (eg restless, agitated, retarded)
Delusions, type of hallucinations

		SCORE	
Orientation	Date		
Time of Day 0: 1: 2			
Day 0: 2			
Date 0: 1			
Month 0: 2			
Year 0: 1			
Place 0: 1: 2			
Full name 0: 1: 2			
Short-term memory at 3 mins.			
John Brown 42 West St. Shirley			
0:1 0:1 0:1 0:1 0:1			
Concentration			
Count to twenty 0: 1			
Backwards from twenty 0: 1: 2			
Count months of year backwards 0: 1: 2			
TOTAL			

Information from GP

History from patient and relatives

Pre-admission self-care ratings

DATE		
Continence—urine		
Continent—find way to toilet		
Dry if toiletted		
Occasionally wet		
Wet		
U.I.A.P.		
I/C at night		
Continence—faeces		
Continent		
Clean if toiletted		
Occasionally soiled		
I/C of faeces		
Night behaviour		
Sleeps well		
Sleeps, quiet 5–6 hours		
Noisy, disturbed		
Wandering, restless		
Day behaviour		
Normal		
Lethargic		
Restless		
Wandering off the ward		
Walking		
Independent		
Independent with frame		
Needs minimal/maximal support		
Immobile		
Dressing/undressing		
Independent		
Needs supervision		
Needs help		
Must be dressed/undressed		
Feeding		
Independent		
Needs adapted equipment		
Needs occasional help		
Must be fed		
Washing, shaving, combing hair		
Independent		
Needs supervision		
Needs help		
Has to be washed, shaved, have hair set, combed		
Falls		
Other problems		

Eyesight		
Glasses		
Hearing		
Aid		
Teeth		
Care		
Get in and out of chair		
Get in and out of bed		
Stairs		
Speech		

For those at home on their own most of the day or living alone

Date		
Cooking		
Shopping		
Money		
Laundry		
Gen. orders		
Cleanliness		

Psychiatric history
Personality traits
  Anxious
  Depressive
  Cyclothymic
  Obsessional
  Suspicious
  Low frustration tolerance
  Violent
  Irresponsible
  Shy
  Loses friends
  Excessive drinking
Previous psychiatric illness

Current medication

Physical examination

Anaemia	Cachexia	Dehydration	Jaundice
Deafness	Blindness	Other features	

Cardiovascular

Pulse rate		Rhythm	BP
Carotid bruits		Periph. pulses	AB
HS		LVF	RVF

Respiratory

Alimentary

Tongue	Teeth
PR	Abdo.

Joints

CNS	*Reflexes*	(R)	(L)
Fundi	B.J.		
Dyspraxia	S.J.		
Cranial	T.J.		
Tremor	Grasp		
Tone	K.J.		
Involuntary movements	A.J.		
Gait	Plantars		
Power			
Sensation			
Other findings			

Main physical abnormalities

Main psychiatric problems

Main physical problems

Investigations needed

Immediate management

Longer term plans & prognosis

Follow-up arrangements

Appendix 2
GUIDELINES FOR COLLABORATION BETWEEN GERIATRIC PHYSICIANS AND PSYCHIATRISTS IN THE CARE OF THE ELDERLY: A PAPER AGREED BY THE STANDING JOINT COMMITTEE OF THE BRITISH GERIATRICS SOCIETY AND THE ROYAL COLLEGE OF PSYCHIATRISTS*

1 Services for the elderly should be unity for 'consumers' (ie patients, families, referrers). Patients should not be bounced back from one part of the service merely because they seem more appropriate for another part; such redistribution of referrals should be the *internal* responsibility of the service.

2 'Unity' does not mean blurring of the specificity of particular professions and facilities within the service, and the patient's right of access to them.

3 Criteria for division of responsibility must be clear, and must be known and accepted both inside and outside the service.

4 Effective collaboration depends on mutual confidence, and often frankly on personal friendships. Trust is indispensable, and people should be able at times to accept each other's judgements about their own responsibilities.

5 Mutual confidence requires basic education in each other's disciplines. Implementation of the sort of reciprocal training schemes which have been proposed at the Standing Joint Committee of the BGS/RC Psych is urgent.

6 The Statutory Instrument for the appointment of consultants allows employing Authorities to invite representation of other relevant specialities on Advisory Appointments Committees. It is always desirable that the local geriatric physician or geriatric psychiatrist should be on the Appointments Committee for his opposite number.

7 *Responsibility should be determined by the assessed needs of the patient,* and not by quirks of referral. For example, if a patient with a gross motor stroke is referred to psychiatrists, he is no less the responsibility of the medical service through having first made contact with the psychiatrists; and vice versa with a patient with severe depression.

8 Lack of resources does not alter the definition of responsibility. Once a patient's needs are recognised as falling within the province of one service, that service should support the patient within the limits of the feasible— even if this is less than ideal; *a 'psychiatric' patient does not become 'geriatric' simply because there are no psychiatric beds, or vice versa.*

9 Despite the foregoing, there are patients who fall in a 'grey' area where they might appropriately be dealt with by either service. This then becomes a matter of negotiation between the two services, but the service which first made contact retains responsibility until ultimate placement is agreed. *Patients must never be allowed to 'fall between two stools'.*

10 The principle that responsibility is determined by the patient's needs applies equally to patients admitted under *compulsory orders.* A patient admitted under the Mental Health Act may occasionally need direct admission to a medical (or surgical) bed, and a patient admitted under the National Assistance Act to a psychiatric bed. The belief that an elderly

*Reprinted from *Organisational and management problems of mental illness hospitals: report of a working group.* DHSS, London, 1980.

patient who is admitted under compulsion will necessarily be disruptive or insist on leaving is understandable, but mistaken. There is rarely difficulty with such patients in general wards.

11   Criteria for division of responsibility in *Services for Mental Illness Related to Old Age* (HM(72)71) are broadly satisfactory though the references there to the presence or absence of 'significant physical disease or illness' may cause difficulties if common sense is not applied.

12   Experience suggests that the best criterion for the placement of demented patients needing longer term care is whether they are *ambulant* or not, always provided there is the flexibility necessary for the odd case that does not fit.

13   'Severe dementia' is used as a criterion in HM(72)71, but this can be misleading if interpreted merely in a cognitive sense. The issue turns on the presence and nature of *behaviour disturbances* associated with dementia and these may be severe in a 'mildly' demented patient, and absent in a 'severely' demented patient.

14   Practice in regard to the establishment of Joint Units, or Psycho-Geriatric Assessment Units as recommended in HM(70)11 varies from district to district. Where geriatric psychiatry and geriatrics are side by side in a District General Hospital it may not be necessary to establish a separate Joint Unit. Joint care does not depend on fixed assignment of joint beds, still less on separate joint units, though these are often desirable, especially when geriatric physician and geriatric psychiatrist have their headquarters in different hospitals. The basic principles of joint care are that patients assessed by one service as needing joint care of both should receive it; that each service should have direct access to joint care; and that 'exit responsibility' should, as in all other situations, depend on the assessed needs of the patient rather than merely on who arranged the original admission.

15   Patients with a psychiatric history who develop physical illness or gross physical deterioration at home, should be reassessed *de novo*. No-one should be labelled as 'a psychiatric patient' by virtue merely of some previous psychiatric episode; and vice versa for patients with previous physical illness who develop psychiatric disorders.

Summary of basic principles

i.   Responsibility is always determined by the need of the patient, rather than by quirks of referral.

ii.   Even when resources are short, as they almost always are, the service in whose responsibility the patient falls must do its best for her; a psychiatric patient does not become 'geriatric' through lack of psychiatric beds.

iii.   In addition to goodwill and good sense, education in each other's disciplines is essential.

iv.   The service must always be a unity for the consumer, though this does not mean blurring of the specific contribution of particular professions and resources within the services, and the patient's right of access to them.

Appendix 3
INTERIM GUIDELINES FOR REGIONAL ADVISORS ON CONSULTANT POSTS IN PSYCHIATRY OF OLD AGE*

The development of an effective psychiatric service for the elderly is dependent upon the allocation of adequate resources. A good candidate, trained in psychiatry for the elderly, is unlikely to consider a post where the provision is inadequate.

The population to be served should be clearly defined as:

a) Total (all ages)
b) Number over 65
c) Number over 75

There should be a description of the type of catchment area in terms of geography and social structure and there should be comment on any aspects of the catchment population which will make the service different from average.

There should be a clear understanding of what facilities are to be allocated to the psychiatrist for the elderly for:

1) Functional illness service for the elderly
2) Dementia service

The DHSS formulae are:

1) *Functional illness service for the elderly* (from within the provision for general psychiatry)

   i) Acute beds 0.5 per 1000 population
   ii) Long stay beds 0.17 per 1000 population
   iii) Day places (to be shared by the inpatient group) 0.65 per 1000 population

2) *Dementia service for the elderly*
   i) *Psychogeriatric assessment unit*—12–20 beds per 250 000 population. This figure is now inadequate because:
      a) Practice has changed from assessment to assessment, treatment and rehabilitation *in situ*.
      b) The proportion of very old people in the population has increased since 1970 (the date of the DHSS recommendation).

   A reasonable figure would be:

   Psychogeriatric unit—1 bed per 1000 population over 65 years. To be on a DGH site.
   ii) *Psychogeriatric long stay*—2.5–3 beds per 1000 population over 65 years.

The equivalent number of long stay patients in a mental hospital, even though they are over 65 years, will not provide vacancies at the necessary rate. The population should be one of genuine elderly severely mentally infirm patients, i.e. severe dementia.

*Reprinted by permission of the Royal College of Psychiatrists from *Bulletin of the RCPsych,* 5, 6, June 1981, 110–111.

iii) *Psychogeriatric day hospital*—3 places per 1000 population over 65 years.

Consultant time

The sessions allocated to old age psychiatry should be seen in the context of the total number of consultant sessions in psychiatry. At present, at least 25% of all psychiatric admissions are over the age of 65. Where an active psychiatric service for the elderly develops, this proportion is likely to increase. For every 10 000 old people in an average community there will be demand for approximately 100 acute psychiatric admissions annually. Because of this high rate of demand and because of the heavy commitment to work in the community, the maximum number of old people for whom one full-time consultant can provide a service will be approximately 22 000. A part-time commitment can be calculated on the basis of 2 000 old people per session.

If an inadequate number of sessions is available to serve the whole of a district's elderly population, inevitably some of the work will remain the responsibility of the general psychiatrists. If this is the case the separate areas of responsibility should be clearly defined by sectorisation. A nebulous commitment to old age psychiatry is easily used by the general psychiatrist as an excuse for refusing to give the psychiatrists for the elderly a fair share of the acute psychiatric facilities.

Non-consultant medical staff

a) *Trainees.* The consultant psychiatrist for the elderly should attract 25% of the psychiatric trainees and these posts should be included in a rotational training scheme. The experience available in this field would be useful for GP trainees who might also be attached to the service.

b) *Senior Registrar.* Experience in psychiatry of the elderly should be available to all senior registrars on a rotational basis. The rapid expansion of consultant posts in psychiatry of the elderly means that training consultants in this field is a primary task and therefore attempts should be made to obtain a senior registrar post specifically for this purpose.

c) *Clinical Assistant.* The service should attract a share of clinical assistant sessions which will reflect the availability of these and the way in which they are used within the psychiatric service.

Secretarial staff

The secretary attached to a consultant psychiatrist for the elderly will have considerable responsibility for management and liaison. If possible she should be employed as a personal secretary with higher clerical grading. 0·5 to 1 full-time secretary will be needed for every 10 000 old people served. A day hospital will need additional receptionist/clerk-typist staffing if it is to work effectively.

134

Community psychiatric nurses for the elderly
1 to 2 nurses per 10 000 population over the age of 65.

Teaching areas
A 50% increase in consultant time will be needed in a teaching area.

There will need to be an increase in all staff if facilities are on several sites.

Other details of the service will be required as follows:
1. *The psychiatric service*
    a) The catchment area (whether or not coterminous with the old age psychiatry catchment area)
    b) Number of acute and long stay beds
    c) Number of sessions of consultant time
    d) Number of trainees
    e) Number of clinical assistant sessions.
    f) Number of day hospital places
    g) Number of community psychiatric nurses

2. *The geriatric service*
    a) The catchment area (whether or not coterminous with the psychiatric service for the elderly)
    b) Total number of consultant sessions
    c) Consultant sessions available to the psychiatric service for the elderly
    d) Total number of geriatric beds
    e) Number of geriatric beds on an acute hospital site
    f) Number of geriatric day hospital places

3. *Social services*
    a) The area served (whether or not coterminous with the health services and the size of the population over 65)
    b) Number of Part 3 residential places and day centre places
    c) Number of EMI home places and EMI day places
    d) Whether or not any personnel are available with special expertise relating to the elderly and the proposed social work input into the psychiatric service for the elderly
    e) Number of places available in private nursing homes
    f) Details of sheltered housing

4. *Administration*
    a) Details of the local cog-wheel organisation
    b) Is there a regional advisor of advisory group in psychiatry of the elderly?

Requirements for a district service with a total population of 200 000 and 30 000 over the age of 65

Functional illness

   i) 15 acute beds
   ii) 5 new long stay beds
   iii) 20 day places

Dementia service

   i) Psychogeriatric unit—30 beds
   ii) Psychogeriatric long stay—75 to 90 beds
   iii) Day places—90

Consultant time

15 sessions.

Non-consultant medical staff

   a) Trainees 25% share of total in psychiatry
   b) Senior Registrar 25% share of total in psychiatry
   c) Clinical Assistants according to availability and deployment.

Secretarial staff

1.5 to 3 secretaries for the functional illness service and the psychogeriatric unit. Additional secretarial time for the dementia day hospital.

Community psychiatric nurses for the elderly

2 to 6 community psychiatric nurses.

In a teaching area there should be a 50% increase in consultant time.

The facilities described above are not ideal but are those required to establish a credible psychiatric service for the elderly. Shortage of money at the present time means that promises made in job descriptions are unlikely to be fulfilled in the short-term and therefore a post should not be approved unless facilities are to be immediately available. Health authorities would be unlikely to create posts for surgeons without beds and operating and anaesthetic facilities. They must be made aware that a psychiatric service likewise cannot operate without a basic provision.